# Preaching Through the Bible

## Genesis 1–11

### Michael A. Eaton

**Sovereign World**

Sovereign World
PO Box 777
Tonbridge
Kent TN11 0ZS
England

By the same author:
*Ecclesiastes* (Tyndale Commentary) – IVP
*The Baptism with the Spirit* – IVP
*How to Live a Godly Life* – Sovereign World
*Living Under Grace* – (Romans 6–7) – Nelson Word
*How to Enjoy God's Worldwide Church* – Sovereign World
*A Theology of Encouragement* – Paternoster
*Preaching Through the Bible* (1 Samuel) – Sovereign World
*Preaching Through the Bible* (2 Samuel) – Sovereign World
*Focus on the Bible*: 1, 2, 3 John – Christian Focus

ISBN: 1 85240 179 6

Typeset by CRB Associates, Reepham, Norfolk
Printed in England by Clays Ltd, St Ives plc.

# Preface

There is need of a series of biblical expositions which are especially appropriate for English-speaking preachers in the Third World. Such expositions need to be laid out in such a way that they will be useful to those who put their material to others in clear points. They need to avoid difficult vocabulary and advanced grammatical structures. They need to avoid European or North American illustrations. *Preaching Through the Bible* seeks to meet such a need. Although intended for an international audience I have no doubt that their simplicity will be of interest to many first-language speakers of English as well.

These expositions will take into account the Hebrew and Greek texts but will also take into account three translations of the Bible, the New King James (or Revised Authorised) Version, the New American Standard Version and the New International Version. The expositions will be comprehensible whichever of these three versions is used, and no doubt with some others as well. At times the expositor will simply translate the Hebrew or Greek himself, as I have done in Genesis chapter 3.

It is not our purpose to deal with minute exegetical detail, although the commentator often has to do work of this nature as part of his preliminary preparation. But just as a housewife likes to serve a good meal rather than display her pots and pans, so the good expositor is concerned with the 'good meal' of Scripture, rather than the 'pots and pans' of dictionaries, disputed interpretations and the like. Only occasionally will such matters have to be discussed. The 'biblical scholar' mentioned in chapter 5 is J.J. Stamm and his essay, 'Die Imago-Lehre von Karl Barth und die alttestamentliche Wissenschaft', in *Antwort: Festschrift Karl Barth*, (ed. E. Wolf and others, Evangelischer Verlag, 1956), pp.84–98. Such 'pots and pans' have been used! However the text is not weighed down with such matters. Similarly matters of 'Introduction' do not receive detailed discussion. A simple outline of some 'introductory' matters will appear in the first chapter of the next book on Genesis. More detailed study may be found elsewhere.

# Contents

# Maps

# Author's Preface

There have been three occasions when I have preached fairly slowly through Genesis. I first preached through Genesis 1–11 on Trans-World Radio some years ago. Then I preached on parts of Genesis (beginning at chapter 12) in Rouxville Baptist church. Later I recorded expositions of Genesis 12–50 and with my earlier broadcasts being repeated, the whole book went out over the air to southern Africa.

Recently I have had another attempt at preaching through selections of Genesis in Nairobi. This little book is the result of the Monday evening meetings of the 'Chrisco Intensive Discipleship School' which took Genesis 1–11 as its book for detailed exposition at the end of 1995 and the beginning of 1996.

I was grateful for the way in which God blessed us at that time. It was a period of intensified blessing. As is our custom we were meeting on four evenings a week. Mondays and Thursday were teaching meetings; Tuesdays and Fridays were 'revival meetings'. At all of them Nairobi City Hall was crowded with some friends having to stand at the doors. These chapters constitute notes on the teaching given on the Mondays during that time.

I am grateful to Jenny Eaton, to Tina Gysling, my daughter, who worked through my material; to my son Calvin who is an ever-present help in time of computer-trouble; and to Chris Mungeam an encourager in Jesus.

# Chapter 1

## Introducing Genesis

Some books of the Bible seem to be more important than others. I do not say they are more inspired by God, but they seem to be more important. Genesis is surely one of the most important books within the pages of Scripture. It is often called 'the book of beginnings' because it tells us of the origin of so many matters which are of importance to us. We read of the origin of the world, the origin of marriage, the origin of sin, of the beginnings of society and of language. Chapters 12 to 50 tell us of the beginnings of the people of God.

To understand anything it is helpful to know its background and its origin. When there is some crisis in some part of the world we ask the questions 'How did that happen? How did that situation arise?' If one of our children gets into difficulty at school, we ask 'What happened? How did this problem originate?' Whether it be a wife, a car, an international crisis, or a fight, we want to know the answer to the question 'How did it begin?' We ask 'Where does this person, event, machine – or whatever – come from? What was its story before it reached me?' We do not feel we understand something until we know the background and the origin.

Genesis asks these questions in the most sweeping way. It addresses questions like 'Where does the universe come from?' 'Where does the human race come from?' 'What is the origin of marriage?' 'Why are there nations?' It is rightly called the book of origins.

**Genesis 1–11 is history written in a child-like parabolic style** (or in the style of a parable). The first three chapters are like stories which we read to children. We read of events that no-one could have witnessed, beginning with the creation of the universe and of the sun and the moon and the stars. We read of the creation of the seas and of animals and of the first man. Startling events are told without the slightest suggestion of anything odd. God works for six days and then takes a day's holiday to enjoy what He has done. A woman is made out of a bone, a snake talks, a tree determines the destiny of the human race, God walks in a garden, another tree can keep humankind alive for ever. It is all strikingly unusual history to say the least!

In Genesis 4 the style of history-writing changes slightly and becomes a little more ordinary. We are approaching more 'normal' history. We read of things like murder and polygamy and jealousy between brothers. We have glimpses of farming and metal-work, music and poetry. This is getting closer to the world we live in. Talking snakes are beyond our experience, but we know about fighting brothers, and men who want more than one woman!

Yet there are still some striking and amazing events. Women start marrying fiendish angels and it leads to such wickedness that God decides to drown the people descending from Cain and Seth and start the human race again. Noah rescues his family by building a boat shaped like a coffin. Animals join him in the boat and so Noah's line is saved, plus its animals. It all seems to be a bit of children's fiction! When the new humanity gets going they all speak the same language, and they decide to build a tower to get to God who apparently lives high up in the sky. God comes down to take a look at what is happening, discovers that the new human race is getting too ambitious and gets them all speaking different languages. It was a good way of bringing an end to their project.

What sort of history-writing is this?

When we get to the end of Genesis 11 the style changes yet more and we are at last into the world that we know about. From Genesis 12 onwards the story is a fairly straightforward narrative of one family which God chose and used to bring the promise of salvation to Israel and to the world. There are still miracles like Isaac being born when his mother is in her nineties, and the dream of the angels who visited Jacob by coming down a staircase, but they are just 'ordinary' miracles compared to Genesis 1–11! Ordinary miracles we can cope with, but Genesis 1–11 definitely has a style of its own!

So I say Genesis 1–11 is history written in a child-like parabolic style. I emphasize both parts of the sentence. (i) It is history. The rest of the Bible treats the characters in Genesis 1–11 as historical. Mesopotamian stories are like this. They tell extravagant tales and yet the characters are undoubtedly historical! The same is true of Genesis 1–11, which uses a style of writing well-known in ancient Mesopotamia. The story-telling has a parabolic style, but the characters are historical. God's inspired word used a Mesopotamian style of history-writing.

(ii) I must emphasize the second half of my sentence above. It is history **written in a child-like parabolic style**. Snakes don't talk, and we know from the New Testament that the snake of Genesis 3 is parabolic. In the book of Revelation the snake is Satan! Yet Satan is not mentioned directly in the book of Genesis. Genesis 3:1 quite clearly talks of the snake being one of the *'animals of the countryside'*.

So the first eleven chapters deal with creation (1:1–2:3) and the original perfection of the human race (2:4–25). Then we have the story of the fall into sin (3:1–6) and the immediate death that came upon the human race (3:7–24). The story then shows us the wider consequences of human sin. Wickedness spread very rapidly. Society was ruined (chapter 4); death ruled everywhere (chapter 5). The human race became subject to demonic powers (6:1–8) and soon had deteriorated so much that God decided to destroy the offspring of Cain and Seth and start again under different conditions. The flood reduced the people to a remnant (6:9–7:24). Then God brought into being a new world out of the waters of the flood (8:1–19), swore that He would never destroy the world in that way again and restarted the world under different conditions (8:20–9:17). Sin and death soon appeared again (9:18–29), but God spread the nations throughout the ancient world (chapter 10) and divided their speech into many languages (11:1–9). The end of Genesis 11 (verses 10–26) shows us the background to the story of Abraham. At the end of chapter 11 we are ready to be introduced to Abraham who will be the model of salvation.

From that point on instead of focusing on the outworking of sin, the story focuses on the one through whom there will come a Saviour, the Seed of Abraham. The remainder of the book shows us how faith works by exhibiting the life of faith in the stories of Abraham (11:27–25:11), Ishmael and Isaac, Jacob and Esau (25:12–36:43), and then in the story of Joseph which is given special attention. Joseph's story shows us how the life of faith works out in one more of Abraham's descendants, but at the same time explains how Israel came to be in Egypt and so in need of salvation by the blood of a lamb.

The start of everything is the fact that God is the Lord of the entire cosmos. It is His world. He made it. He tells us how it works. He claims the right to say how we should live. And He alone can put the race right when it goes astray. Creation is the start of everything. In the beginning God created the heavens and the earth.

# Chapter 2

## In the Beginning
### (Genesis 1:1)

The first thing we need to know about our origins is that God is there, God is real, God is unique, and God is the Lord and Master of everything. All of this is taught in the very first verse of the Bible.

It is not an accident that the Bible begins in the way it does. The fact that God is there as the Creator of the universe is the start of all healthy thinking, all true worship, and it is the starting point of true godliness.

Genesis 1:1 to 2:3 is the story of the creation of the world. God is pictured as a workman who works for six days and then rests for a seventh day. Genesis 1:1 is not a title for the section, but is rather the opening sentence of verses 1–5.

We must look at Genesis 1:1 carefully, considering its wording, its teaching and its implication for our lives.

1. Consider first **the wording of Genesis 1:1**. *'In the beginning God created the heavens and the earth.'*

*In the beginning...* It does not say in the beginning 'of' anything. It simply talks about 'the' beginning. It is an absolute beginning. This phrase comes also in John 1:1 *'In the beginning the Word was already there...'* It refers to the beginning of everything, before history, as far back as your mind can imagine.

*God...* This is the first time the word 'God' is used in the Bible. It is worth noticing that the names and words for God are often used in a careful way. The word 'God' is the ordinary word that even unbelieving people use. Its meaning is defined here. 'God', in the rest of the Bible, means 'the God of creation', the Creator of the universe. Later when we see God interacting with men and women, we shall find a different word being used, the word 'Yahweh' or 'LORD'. But 'God' is the common and ordinary word, meaning the mighty One who created us. 'God' is a word that stresses God's power. It takes its meaning from this chapter.

The first mention of God in the Bible refers to what He does. The Bible does not give any abstract, philosophical ideas about God. God is not known apart from what He does and what He says. The only God is the God of the Bible, the God of creation, the God of Abraham, the God who came in Jesus. From Genesis 1:1 onwards this word 'God' will mean 'the sovereign creator-God who revealed Himself in Israel'. Later on the term 'Yahweh' will be used, more with reference to salvation. It means 'the God who redeems by the blood of a lamb'. But here Genesis 1:1 introduced God as the creator-God.

*Created...* The Bible only uses the word 'create' with God as the subject. It never has any man or woman as a subject. It never says any person 'created' anything. Nowadays we often speak of people being 'creative'. It is alright to speak that way but we ought to notice that the Bible specially reserves the word 'create' for things that only God can do.

Then the word is always used of something happening which is new and extraordinary. Also, we note that the word is never used mentioning any kind of material being used. God does not create 'out of' something else. 'Create' means 'bring into existence without using pre-existing

material'. The word is used of other things besides creating
the world. It is also used of God's work of salvation
(2 Corinthians 5:17). New life is also 'created' when a
person is in Christ.

*The heavens and the earth*. This is a way of saying
'absolutely everything'. When you get a pair of words like
this, 'heavens ... earth', it is a Hebrew way of expressing
totality. The phrase 'from Dan to Beersheba' means
'throughout all Israel from the north to the south'. This
making an expression out of a pair of opposite words is a
way of saying 'every single thing that there is', the heavens
(what we see when we look up) and the earth (what we see
when we look down) and everything in between.

2. Consider next **the teaching of Genesis 1:1**.

We notice first that God's existence is taken for granted.
The Bible never tries to prove the existence of God. All
people know that God is real. The Bible simply starts
talking about Him. *'In the beginning God...'*.

Genesis 1:1 excludes the idea that matter is eternal. The
stuff this world is made of has not always existed. Material
things, the elements of the universe, once did not exist.

It teaches that God created everything from nothing,
that is, without using pre-existing material. Everything that
there is, is created by God.

It contradicts pantheism, the idea that everything is
God, and that the universe is divine. Pantheism is not
true. We must never worship the world. *'In the beginning,
God created...'*. There is a distinction between God and
the stuff of which the universe is made. In the beginning
God was there, but the heavens and the earth were not
there. God created them.

God is utterly self-sufficient. God once did not have
anything there other than Himself. *'The God who made the
world and all the things in it, the One who is Lord of heaven
and earth ... is not served by human hands as though He*

*needed anything. He is the One who gives to everyone life and breath and everything'* (Acts 17:24–25). God does not need anything outside of Himself. He depends on nothing; everything depends upon Him.

3. Consider next **the wider implications of Genesis 1:1**.

This verse gives us the background to the rest of the Bible. This is the background to everything we need to know about sin, about redemption, about history, about the future.

God created us. This means that God has rights over us. The reason why sin is sin is that God is our Maker. He has sovereign rights over this universe. Any person who lives out of touch with His creator is rebelling against the One who knows everything and can do anything with the world He made.

This is the background to God's ability to control the world. The reason why God can control this world is because He is the One who made it in the first place. He knows how it works. The laws of nature are His laws. This verse gives us the background to redemption. Salvation is God doing something about His world. When this world fell into sin and darkness, God was not willing to let it go. God is saving the world that He made in the beginning.

This verse means that God is capable of handling our lives. Imagine you have some machine, and then it goes wrong. What do you do? Eventually you might have to say, 'Let us send it back to the one who made it. Back to the maker!' But it is this way with us. God made us. Yet we have become broken. Is there any answer? Yes, the answer is 'Back to the Maker!' He is the One who knows how we function. He knows what is good for us. He knows what is bad for us. If we wish to function aright in this world, we must follow the Maker's instructions, the way He designed the world and the way He designed us.

When God sent Jesus He was making a way for His world
to come back to Him. Out of the old fallen world which
He made, He brings into being a new creation
(2 Corinthians 5:17). The new creation is His determina-
tion not to abandon the old creation. Because God is
Creator, He is able to be Saviour.

# *Chapter 3*

# Preparing the World for Humankind
(Genesis 1:2–3)

Immediately after Genesis 1:1 the Bible narrows down. The rest of the section focuses very definitely on the earth. The Hebrew emphasizes the word 'earth' and can be translated 'Now as for the earth – it was without form and empty' (Genesis 1:2). Genesis is not about to tell us much about the other stuff of the universe mentioned in Genesis 1:1. It does not have any special mention of angels at this point. It zooms in on the special area of concern – the earth.

In this picturesque description, the world is created in two stages. First the elementary 'stuff' is made, but that leaves the earth *'without form and empty'*. Then Genesis 1:3–31 tells us of how God arranged and ordered the world.

The point is that God was getting the world ready for the human race. Verse 2 does not refer to chaos, but to emptiness, which is not quite the same. And it is not possible to translate verse 2 *'And the earth **became** without form and empty...'*. The Hebrew for this would be different. 'Became' is an unnatural translation.

The main point of verse 2 is that the world had to be developed. The direction of the development indicates that it was being designed for the human race.

*'Without form'* means undeveloped, like a blank chalkboard, without anything on it. *'Empty'* means that it had no people there. *'Yahweh, who created the heavens and the earth ... did not create it formless ... He formed it to be inhabited...'* (Isaiah 45:18). It was 'formless' at first but then God remedied the lack and it became inhabited. The point of Genesis 1:2 is that the earth was not ready for inhabitants.

Genesis continues *'... and darkness was over the surface of the waters'*. The picture is of a liquid world. It was totally unsuitable for men and women. It was enveloped in darkness. People need solid ground. People need light.

The point of verse 2 is to underline the fact that in Genesis 1:3–31 God is shaping and moulding the world for the human race. Genesis 1:3–31 will be the story of how God makes the planet earth a suitable place for man to dwell in. Hebrews 2:5–6 makes a similar point. *'God did not subject the world to come* – the earth when it is finally glorified – *to angels ... But someone has testified somewhere, saying, "What is man, that you remember him...".'* The earth was not for angels; it was for the human race. Light is needful for man. Ground is needed instead of seas. There has to be provision of rain. An 'expanse' has to come into being, the sky. Everything is being described from the viewpoint of men and women. In Genesis 1:29 vegetation is specifically for people. The sun and moon are for people to tell the time. The animals are for humankind (Genesis 1:26) and are specially close to them (1:25–26). The 'rest' of Genesis 2:1–3 prefigures spiritual rest for people.

How did this shaping of creation for the human race take place? It involved the Holy Spirit, the 'breath' of God. Genesis continues: *'and the Spirit of God was moving over the surface of the waters'*. God used His Holy Spirit to prepare the world for the human race. This first reference to the Holy Spirit in the Bible gives us an idea of what the Holy Spirit will always do. He is the One who gives life, the One who gives form and shape and direction to our lives. He is the One who gives shape and order to creation, the agent through whom creation was adorned. He was like a bird hovering over a nest, waiting to see the eggs burst forth with life.

The adornment and preparation of creation also takes place by God's speaking. *'And God said, "Let there be light"; and there was light'.* Creation takes place through God's word. He speaks and things happen. *'By the word of the LORD the heavens were made; by the breath of His mouth all their parts were formed'* (Psalm 33:6).

It is interesting that salvation also follows a similar pattern to what we find here. When God first comes to us He finds our lives empty and without shape or purpose. Then He works in our lives. His Spirit moves upon us. His word comes to us. This is not simply a piece of fancy 'spiritualizing' on my part. This is the way Paul considers the matter. *'The God who said, "Light shall shine out of darkness" is the One who has shone in our hearts to give the light of the knowledge of the glory of God in the face of Christ'* (2 Corinthians 4:6).

God's ways of working in creation and in salvation are similar. Salvation is His restoration of creation, using a similar pattern. God comes to us in our emptiness. He finds us in darkness, emptiness, hopelessness. His creative word brings life to us. If anyone gets to be *'in Christ'*, there is a new creation (2 Corinthians 5:17). Creation from nothing is one of the patterns of God's action. *'He calls into being that which does not exist'* (Romans 4:17). He works by His Spirit. He speaks. And the very universe comes into being by His word. What He did at first He can do again in a thousand ways. He has but to say a word and nothing becomes something, light becomes darkness, emptiness becomes expectation. God has acted. When He acts He brings newness, light, and solid ground – in more ways than one.

# Chapter 4

# The Glory of God in Creation
## (Genesis 1:3–31)

Genesis 1:3–31 describes how God shaped the earth in six 'days' of activity. It is not mythology. Creation is taken seriously by the New Testament (Hebrews 11:3; 2 Peter 3:5; 2 Corinthians 4:6; Acts 17:24) and it was taken seriously by Jesus (Matthew 19:4). It is not poetry. It does not have in it many characteristics of poetry. There is some 'parallelism' in Genesis 1:26, but there is no rhyme in Genesis 1, and no metre.

Days 1 to 3 are prior to the sun, which defines what a 'day' is. John 5:17 and Hebrews 4:10–11 imply that day 7 is still continuing, so day 7 has certainly lasted more than 24 hours! And then Genesis 2 tells the story of the creation of man and woman in fuller detail, and it tells the story in a way that shows Genesis 1 is non-literal. The events of the sixth day as described in Genesis 2 take more than a day. Genesis 1:30 gives impression of 'nature' in ordinary non-miraculous activity. All of this implies that the days were not meant to be taken as literal 24–hour periods.

Some, like the great 'Saint Augustine', have thought the 'days' of Genesis are ages. Some have believed that the days are literal but there are gaps in between. Some have believed that the 'days' are days of revelation, not days in which creation took place but days in which God spoke to

Moses about what happened (but there is no hint of anything like this in the text, and Exodus 20:11 is against it).

I am more interested in the teaching of Genesis than in getting over-anxious about how Genesis fits with science. I agree with John Calvin who said 'Let him who would learn astronomy and other obscure arts go somewhere else!'

Genesis is describing facts but it is using picture language. It is written so simply a child could enjoy it – and many have. It depicts God as a workman, the model for the way we should work (note Exodus 20:11). It seems God created the world in six creative periods and this is put to us in terms of a picture of God as a workman.

It is not 100% in chronological order. Almost certainly the writer puts things in groups more than in strict chronology. The stars are mentioned at an appropriate point, but the date of their origin cannot be deduced from Genesis. One need not worry about clashes with a scientific account. It is not intended as a scientific description at all.

Notice that Genesis 1:1–31 has a beautiful structure to it.

### The Whole (1:1–2)

| | |
|---|---|
| Day 1: Light (1:3–5) | Day 4: Light bearers (1:14–19) |
| Day 2: Dividing waters (1:6–8) | Day 5: Birds and sea creatures (1:20–23) |
| Day 3: Land and water (1:9–10); vegetation (1:11–13) | Day 6: Land animals and reptiles (1:24–25); man (1:26–31) |

### Rest (2:1–4)

We are surely not meant to press the details of Genesis into harmony with science. Genesis 1 is like a vision.

26

Maybe – but we do not know for sure – someone received it as vision. We miss the point if we treat it like an astronomical textbook. Certainly the minute details of the chronology are not meant to be taken scientifically.

Genesis 1:3–31 is a wonderful description of the glory of God. Let me try to bring out some of its highlights

1. **Our creator-God is the only God**. Everything else is created by Him. God created the heaven and the earth. Many things mentioned in this chapter were treated as gods by the people of the ancient world. In some places the Creator and 'the deep' were rival gods. In other places light and darkness were gods. In some places the sea is a god. Yet it was God who created the seas, and separated them from the land. There were many fertility gods in the ancient world, but God is the source of fertility (note Genesis 1:22). Some ancient peoples worshipped the sun or the moon or the stars. Astrologers still worship the stars as a source of knowledge! But these things were all made by God. They are not gods; they are 'things' made by God. Many nations have viewed animals as gods. Some have worshipped the cow or the bull or other animals (see Romans 1:22, 23). Genesis 1 sets itself against all idolatry.

2. **God is the only creator**. The phrases in the Hebrew express totality: light and darkness; earth and sea; water above and below the sky; sun and moon; herbs and trees. Nothing in creation creates itself. Everything is from God. He is the only one who is eternal. The creator is the only God; only God is the creator.

3. **Creation is good**. The chapter tells us of the goodness of creation. It is emphasized again and again (Genesis 1:4, 10, 12, 18, 21, 25, 31). Wherever evil comes from, it was not built into the original creation. It must be a good thing gone wrong. Some philosophers have said that 'matter' is evil; that the physical fabric of the world is somehow an evil thing and only non-material 'spirit' is good. Even the

27

church was tempted to follow this pagan thinking at times. It led to things like clerical celibacy and similar asceticism (see 1 Timothy 4). But sin is not in matter; it is not built into creation as its essence.

4. **Creation reveals the wisdom and purposefulness of God**. Creation is designed for men and women. Light is required by human beings. Men and women need to tell the times and the seasons. The sun and the moon were put there to help him. Man needs rain, land, food. All were designed for him.

Because creation came into being from God, the world is basically reliable. Day and night continue steadily. There is regularity in nature. The seasons show order. This is the basis of science. Plants and animals bear offspring after their kinds. This is the basis of agriculture and animal husbandry. Imagine what life would be like if animals did **not** bear offspring after their kind.

Creation shows great variety. Among the animals, in vegetable-life, among men and women, in each case there is great variety. No human being is identical to another human being. No tree is identical to another tree. In each case there are small and large. There are fish for the sea, and birds for the air, and other types of animals for the land. What variety and complexity is there.

There is beauty in creation. God is a great artist. God Himself enjoys the goodness of creation (see Psalm 104; Proverbs 3:19; 8:22).

5. **Creation reveals the personality and the graciousness of God**. It implies that God is a person; God is 'he', not 'it'. It shows God's love for man. Everything was designed for humankind, not for angels, It all shows God's grace. He did not have to do any of this. He does not need us in the way that we need Him (Acts 17:24, 25). It all shows God exercising His loving power. It all happened according to His will. He said *'Let there be . . . '* and there was. The

words '*It was so*' come throughout the chapter (1:3, 7, 9, 11, 15, 24, 30).

What then does creation mean to us? Every Christian should love creation and enjoy it. If pagans worship nature in idolatry we should worship God for it. It is of the essence of wisdom to know about creation. Solomon's wisdom involved a study of creation (1 Kings 4:33). Solomon grew steadily in his knowledge of creation (see Proverbs 1:27; 5:19; 6:5, 6–11). He learned lessons about life from even the ants (Proverbs 7:22, 23; 25:13; 26:1–3, 9, 11; 27:8; 28:1, 15; 30:15, 19, 31). We are to glory in the God of creation. The heavens declare the glory of God.

# Chapter 5

# The Image of God
### (Genesis 1:26–27)

At Genesis 1:26 the narrative slows down. Everything in Genesis chapter 1 leads up to this point and the story then becomes unhurried and gives greater detail. We notice that only in the case of the creation of mankind do we have a special mention of God's counsel. It is a way of saying that God shows special interest in the human race.

**Then God said, *'Let us make man as our image, according to our likeness'*** (Genesis 1:26). There is no special distinction between the words 'image' and 'likeness'. Only the term 'image' is in verse 27. In verse 26 the two words simply support each other by saying the same thing twice with two similar words. Also the change, *'as ... according to'*, has no special significance. In 5:1 we have 'as' with the word 'likeness'.

What is this 'image of God'? Each age tends to read its own ideas into the 'image of God'. In the fifth century a 'church father' called Athanasius was interested in Jesus as the 'Logos' (Word, reason). He said the image of God was our ability to reason. Augustine was interested in God as trinity, as Father, Son and Holy Spirit. He said the image of God was the 'trinity' in man consisting of memory, affection, and will. In the 16th century the 'Reformers' who were used by God to bring revival to the church were interested in justification by faith only. They said the image of God was man's original righteousness before the fall of Adam. At the 'Enlightenment', a time of European history when there was special emphasis on human ability, scholars said the 'image of God' was the enlightened soul of man. Karl Barth, a twentieth-century theologian, lived in a day when interaction between people was causing much interest. He said the image of God was relationship between sexes. Each age interprets 'the image' in terms of its own interests!

Half a century ago a biblical scholar summarised people's opinons about the image of God. He put the various opinions into four groups. (i) One group consists of those who think the image of God is some spiritual quality in man, such as self-consciousness, understanding of the eternal, capacity for thought, personality, vitality. (ii) Another group contained those who thought the image of God had a connection with rule over creation. (iii) A third approach stressed direct relationship with God, (iv) and a fourth group stressed physical shape.

So obviously the 'image of God' is a subject where there are a lot of different opinions. How are we going to tackle the matter? I suggest we can come at it in four ways: by considering the New Testament use of Genesis 1:26, 27; by considering the description of God in Genesis 1:1–24; by considering the words of Genesis 1:26–27 carefully; and by considering how 'images' were used in the ancient world.

1. **One way of considering the image of God is to remind ourselves how the idea is used in the New Testament**. When we look at New Testament passages of Scripture, how do they interpret the image of God?

Judging by the New Testament, the image of God is true knowledge of God; it is righteousness and holiness. This is the point of Colossians 3:10 and Ephesians 4:24. It is a capacity for personal relationships. James 3:9–10 (recalling Genesis 9:6) treats sin against fellow man as enormous because of the image of God. It is a capacity for a progressive relationship to God. Romans 8:29 says that Christians are predestined to be conformed to the image of Jesus. 2 Corinthians 3:18 says by our knowing God through Jesus we are to be transformed more and more into His likeness. Romans 12:1–2 says something similar. Also, judging by the New Testament the image of God is a capacity for ruling God's world. This is why 1 Corinthians chapter 11 which has much to say about degrees of authority, brings in the subject of the image of God.

2. **Another way of considering the image of God is to recall how God has been described in Genesis 1:1–25**. When Genesis 1:26 talks about the image of God, it has of course been talking of God for the previous twenty-five verses. So what is it in verses 1–25 that is true of God but also is characteristic of men and women.

In Genesis 1, God is personal. He makes decisions concerning creation. He expresses ideas within Himself. He is able to contemplate what He does. Man's nature also comprises these things. Men and women think, reflect. They interact with others. They have a capacity for speech and thought and communication with each other. They are capable of personal relationships. Men and women are able to consider the world around them. God gave names to aspects of creation. In Genesis 2:20 Adam names things. Men and women are the image of God in their capacity to think and analyse.

In Genesis 1, God is holy and righteous. He makes good things. Part of the image of God is man's original goodness (see Colossians 3:10; Ephesians 4:24). Holiness and righteousness are part of God's image. God was holy and righteous. When He made men and women He made people who in some respects were like Himself. They were created good.

In Genesis 1, God is a ruler and a king. The ruling function of men and women is part of the image, or the immediate result of his being the image of God. Genesis 1:28 follows immediately on Genesis 1:25, 26. Ruling over creation is a task delegated to man (see Psalm 8:6). This does not mean that the human race must exploit creation excessively like a tyrant. In the Bible 'ruling' and 'shepherding' are closely related. Man rules over creation by being a good shepherd of creation.

In Genesis 1, God is a creator. Similarly creativity is part of human character. Man is to draw out capabilities of nature. Man has a capacity for skilful and creative use of what he finds in God's world. The vision of the glory of God which we have in Genesis 1:1–25 and even into 1:28–2:3 shows us something of what it means for men and women to be God-like, made as the image of God.

Men and women are also like God in being designed to *'enter into rest'*, but we shall come back to that below.

## *Chapter 6*

# Representing God

(Genesis 1:26–31)

**3. A third way of considering the image of God is to study Genesis 1:26 as fully as we can**. God says *'Let us make man as our image, according to our likeness'*.

First of all we may note that we should not speak of humankind being 'in' the image of God. God made man 'as' the image of God.[1] This is important. It is the **whole** person who is the image of God. It is not that men and women are 'in' anything. It deals with what they **are**. They **are** the image of God.

The word 'image' includes the idea of 'shape'. It may seem strange to say that men and women are made as the shape of God! But the word 'image' does include the idea of shape! The word 'image' has spatial properties in Old Testament usage and includes the idea of physical form.

We know that *'God is spirit'*. He does not have a body; He is not material. Yet we also know that there were times when God took on a visible appearance. He was causing something to be visible which represented Himself. It was not that people were seeing God, but they were seeing what represented God. When God did this and appeared in visible form, in Old Testament times, He always took the shape of a man (see Judges 13:21, 22; Ezekiel 1:26, 28). When the Bible says that man is the image of God it includes man's body. 'Image' means shape. God does not have a body (see Deuteronomy 4:12; Isaiah 40:18) but there is a shape that is appropriate to God (Ezekiel 1:26). Our human 'shape' is God's 'shape' first. It does not mean that God has a body, but it does mean that there was a shape that God chose to use. The whole man is the image of God; it includes the body!

Genesis 1:26 speaks of man as the image of God. It does not talk of **part** of man being in the image of God. It certainly does not talk of the 'soul' as being in the image of God. And certainly the image of God is not the 'immortality of the soul'.

4. **A fourth way of considering the image of God is to remember how 'images' were used in the ancient world**. In the thinking of the ancient Near East images were representations of a king or of a god. A king might have a statue of himself set up in a temple. Symbolically it meant that he was ever in the presence of his god praying to it. Sometimes the king himself would be thought to be the living 'image' of the god he worshipped. This kind of thinking was familiar to the first readers of Genesis. The point of this for us is that we are God's representatives, His living image here in His world. Let us now come to consider what this teaching about 'the image of God' ought to mean to us.

1. **It helps us to understand the second commandment**. The reason why Israel was forbidden to make an image of God is because the human race itself is to be the image of God.

2. **It helps us to understand what sin is**. It is falling from the glory of God. It is damaging the original righteousness in which God created the human race. After man fell the image was damaged. New human beings were more the image of Adam than the image of God (Genesis 5:3). Yet

the image is not totally lost (see James 3:9 which implies man is still the image of God).

3. **It helps us to understand why life is sacred**. The fact that man is the image of God makes murder a very serious sin (see Genesis 9:6). Capital punishment was required as a punishment for murder.

4. **We must remember that both men and women are the image of God**. Genesis says *'Let them rule ... '*. The earth is given to man for him to care for. Genesis 1:28 comes to both men and women (although 1 Corinthians 11 says that in the matter of authority the image functions under man).

5. **Jesus is the perfect image of God**. Only He is the perfect man. He is fully God's image (see John 12:45; 14:9; 2 Corinthians 4:4; Colossians 1:15; Hebrews 1:3).

6. **One day the image will be perfectly restored in God's people**. Man will be fully restored to the image of God (see 1 Corinthians 15:49). He will have perfect dominion. Psalm 8 will be fulfilled. 1 Corinthians 6:3 will come to pass.

It begins now. Man now is to be the image of God. The possibility is still open to him. The process of getting back to being the representative of God starts when we have fellowship with the Lord Jesus Christ (2 Corinthians 3:18). Progressively we get to be like Jesus.

After telling us about the image of God (Genesis 1:26–27), Genesis 1:28–31 goes on to tell us how the human race was given commands concerning procreation and dominion (1:28). Food is provided for him (1:29; meat would be provided later). Vegetable food is given also to the animals (1:30). The whole of creation is said to be good (1:31).

It is worth noticing the difference between human beings and the animals. They have a lot in common. Man and the animals (i) share the same day; (ii) were both created from the dust (Genesis 1:24; 2:7; 3:19). (iii) They have much in common in their functioning, as we see in Genesis 1:22 and 28. A difference is in the words *'said unto them'*. God talks to the human race; He does not talk to the animals! (iv) They have a digestive system in common, feeding habits in common. They both maintain life with food (Genesis 1:28, 30; 2:7). (v) Each reproduces after its kind. This is not mentioned explicitly, but it is implied. (vi) Both are said to be 'living being'. Man has something in common with inanimate nature. He is made of the dust of the ground. Man has something in common with animate nature. He has many resemblances to the animals. What then makes men and women unique? They are made in the image of God.

## Footnote

[1] It uses what scholars call the **beth essentiae**, a preposition meaning 'as'.

# Chapter 7

## God's Rest

### (Genesis 2:1–3)

After seven 'days' of creation, God is pictured as 'resting'. First we consider **what God's seventh-day rest meant to Him**. It was a time when God was enjoying looking at what He had done. God's resting is not idleness or inactivity. At every stage of creation God had reviewed what He had done, and at each point God *'saw that it was good'* (Genesis 1:4, 10, 12, 18, 21, 25). Then at the end of the six days God saw everything that He had done and it was all exceedingly good. God's rest is the continuation of Genesis 1:31. It is the immediate effect of His having laboured for six days. God's rest is God's 'reward' for what He had done.

God's rest is still continuing. It is possible for us to 'enter' it even now (Hebrews 4:11). In Genesis, although we are told of the end of each of the six days (Genesis 1:5, 8, 13, 19, 23, 31) we are not told of the end of the seventh day. It has not ended!

God's rest is not idleness. Jesus once healed a man on the Sabbath, and the Jews criticized Him. Their idea was that the Sabbath was a day for doing nothing! Jesus replied *'My Father is **working** . . . '* (John 5:17). God's days of creating the universe have finished; now God is on His long period of Sabbath-rest. But it is not idleness. God is still at work. He can heal a person. God's Sabbath is His joy in what He has done. It is His reaping the benefit of His previous activity. It is His entering into the blessing of the six day's work.

Next, we consider **the spiritual experience of entering into rest**. The Bible tells us that it is possible to *'enter into'* God's rest. What does it mean to *'enter into rest'* in this way?

There is a spiritual experience that corresponds to God's Sabbath. When God made the world and was enjoying what He had done, His plan was that man, having been made at the end of the six days, should *'enter into'* what God had done. God had done all the creating. Man was now to come along and enter into it all. The human race was designed to *'enter into God's rest'* that is to reap the benefit of everything that God had done in making His perfect world.

*'Entering into rest'* is the reward that comes to the Christian in this life as a result of diligent and persistent faith. It is the joy of inheriting promises. It is experiencing the oath of God, when He swears that He will bless us. It is when after years, maybe, of persistent faith, we come to have an assurance that we have obtained that which we have been looking for and which God has promised us.

If man had continued in obedience, the reward for his obedience would have been perfect enjoyment of everything that God had created for him. But man lost the privilege of entering into this rest of God. He rebelled. He became a sinner, and the possibility of enjoying with God everything that God had done was lost for the human race. It can be restored only by persistent and obedient faith in Jesus.

*'Entering into rest'* is what happened to Abraham when after years of diligent faith and testing, God said to him *'Now I see you fear me ...'* At that point **on God's side** an

oath was taken. At that point on **Abraham's side**, he entered into rest. At that point the promise was 'obtained'. Before that point it could have been aborted.

*'Entering into rest'* is what happened to David when after years of trials and tribulations he finally came to the point where God took an oath, and without the possibility of any reversal said to David *'Your seed will continue for ever. I swear it!'* (if I may summarise 2 Samuel 7 and Psalm 89 in this way). On God's side an oath was taken. On David's side after many struggles against many enemies *'The Lord had given him rest on every side'* (2 Samuel 7:1). God also gave him rest within by giving an unshakable oath that his seed would last for ever.

When a Christian comes to the point of believing obedience, it is **God's rest** that he enters into. He *'ceases from his own labours'* and enjoys reaping the benefit of what God has done, just as at the time of creation, God did all the work and man entered into what He had done.

Next, we consider **what the Sabbath meant to Israel**. The word 'Sabbath' means stoppage or cessation or standstill. Just before Israel got to Mount Sinai, God gave them a little training in *'keeping the Sabbath'* (Exodus 16:22–30). It had never been kept before. (Genesis 2:1–3 says nothing at all about any person *'keeping the Sabbath'*.) Then a few months later God gave the nation of Israel a command to keep Saturday as a holy day (Exodus 20:8–11). There was a social reason for it; it gave people a rest (Exodus 23:12). It was a 'sign' that God was in special relationship with Israel. The death penalty was the punishment for not keeping it (Exodus 31:12–17). From time to time people were reminded of its importance (Exodus 34:21; 35:2–3; Leviticus 19:3, 30; 23:3; 26:2).

The main reason for the Sabbath seems to have been to make it clear that **God has a divine timetable**. He created the human race to bring everyone into *'enjoying His rest'*.

The sin of man held up the plan for centuries. But God has a programme to reintroduce the possibility of enjoying His rest. That plan involved the nation of Israel. Israel had to keep the Sabbath as a sign that they were part of the programme of God to bring spiritual rest to the entire world. The law demanded it be kept, under threat of the death penalty for disobedience.

When Jesus came the legal side of the matter was dropped. The Christian is not under Israel's law. It is still true that to take a holiday one day in seven is often a good idea, but there is no longer any law about it. A person can *'consider all days alike'* if he wishes (Romans 14:5). What matters now is not that we 'keep the law of Moses' but that we enter into God's enjoyment of what He is doing. By diligent faith we are to *'enter into rest'* by reaching the point where God is pleased with us, and gives us an oath that He will bless us.

Lastly, it may be necessary to consider **Sunday, and how it relates to the Sabbath**. It does not relate to it at all! Sunday is not a Sabbath. The Christians kept Sunday to make it clear they were **not** keeping the **Saturday-Sabbath** of the Mosaic law. The Christian is released from the Mosaic law; he fulfils it by being under the guidance of the Holy Spirit.

Sunday is a matter of convenience. In the days of the New Testament it was convenient to keep Sunday as a day of worship. It was the day Jesus rose from the dead and so it could be called 'the Lord's day'. The keeping of days is a matter of convenience, of helpful tradition. It is not a matter of law.

The way to 'keep the Sabbath' is not to have exaggerated ideas about Sunday. The way to keep the Sabbath is to give diligence to enter into God's rest.

# Chapter 8

## The Nature of Man

### (Genesis 2:4–7)

A new major section in the book of Genesis begins by saying *'These are the sequel of the heavens and the earth when they were created; in the time when Yahweh God made the earth and the heavens'*. It will be noticed that this sentence says the same things twice; and that the order is reversed.

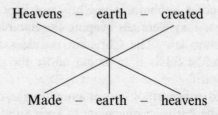

Heavens — earth — created

Made — earth — heavens

This style of saying the same thing twice is an ancient form of internal heading. The section begins at the beginning of verse 4, not (as in the paragraphing of some Bibles) at Genesis 2:4b.

The word 'generations' or (as I translate it) 'sequel' or 'descendants' is an important word. It refers to the 'product' or 'offspring' of something. This section of Genesis deals with the things that **issue forth** from the creation. So now in Genesis 2:4 to 4:26 we have what immediately **follows**, what **arises from**, the heavens and the earth.

There are ten places in the book of Genesis (Genesis 2:4; 5:1; 6:9; 10:1; 11:10; 11:27; 25:12; 25:19; 36:1; 37:2) where we have the word 'descendants' or 'sequel' used as an internal heading. It is like the chapter heading of a modern book. The book of Genesis has a preface and then is followed by ten major sections. The word itself means 'what comes after' or 'something that is generated by something else'. What comes after the heading refers to the **next** stage. The 'generation' of heavens and earth is about what **emerges** from them. The story of Abraham is called 'The Descendants of Terah'.

There was a narrowing down in Genesis 1:2 after Genesis 1:1. The story moved from 'heavens and earth' to earth alone. Now there is a further 'narrowing down'. First we had the whole cosmos (1:1). Then we had the earth (1:2–2:3). Now Genesis 2:4–25 shows a narrower perspective and comes to deal in fuller details with humankind. It was told in summary in Genesis 1:26–27; now the story of the creation of man and woman is told in fuller detail.

Two main points stand out in these verses. (1) **God's world was designed for humankind**. Consider Genesis 2:5–6. Originally the earth was unsuitable for men and women. These verses are like Genesis 1:2 in showing that the world had to be specially prepared for humankind. Verse 5 shows the world was unsuitable for the human race because there was no vegetation, no rain, no cultivation. Verse 6 shows how God prepared the world for men and women. He began by sending some kind of flood to irrigate the earth and make it possible to be farmed.

The next thing that stands out is (2) that **the human person consists of two elements**. We have a physical, material side to our nature. And we have an inner personality. Consider Genesis 2:7. The man was made of the physical elements of the earth. Humankind has a relationship with the physical environment. We also have something in common with the animals. Because we are made in the image of God, we have something in common with God also.

The human person consists of two elements. There is something physical and something not physical, breathed into us by God. This 'personality' or 'breath of God' is sometimes (but rarely) called the 'soul' in the Bible. For example in Matthew 10:28 we have this kind of language. But it must be noticed that here in Genesis 2:7 the 'soul' or 'living being' is the **whole** man, not a part of him. (The language of the Bible is not 'jargon' or technical vocabulary. The word 'soul' in the Bible is used in many different ways. It can even mean a dead person or a corpse, as in Numbers 19:11 which refers to the *'dead body of any soul'*, that is, *'... of any person'*! 'Soul' is not a technical term in the Bible.) Without using particular technical words the entire Bible teaches that man consists of body and personality (see Ecclesiastes 12:7; Matthew 10:28; 26:41; 27:50; Luke 8:55; Acts 2:26, 27, 31; Romans 7:22–23, 24, 25; 8:10, 13; 12:1–2; 1 Corinthians 4:16; 5:5; 7:34; 9:27; 13:3; 2 Corinthians 5:1–8; 2 Corinthians 7:1; 12:2, 3; Ephesians 2:3; James 2:26 and elsewhere). The teaching comes in complete sentences not in particular technical words. Two elements go to make up the person. Paul says that 'he' desires to depart and be with Christ but that 'he' is likely to remain *'in the body'* (Philippians 1:22). Part of us comes from an earthly father and part of us comes from a heavenly creator, the 'father of spirits' (Hebrews 12:9). The Bible occasionally draws a distinction between soul and spirit (1 Thessalonians 5:23 and Hebrews 4:12 are sometimes quoted), but these are not 'parts' of man. They are different aspects of the whole human personality.

Mark 12:33 speaks of 'heart ... understanding ... soul ... strength' but these are not four **parts** of a human being. Nor are there three **parts** of a human being in 1 Thessalonians 5:23. Genesis 2:7 is clear. There are two 'ingredients' in the human person. Most of the time they are tightly integrated. In death, body and personality separate. In having 'breath of life', a living personality from God, man becomes a unified living being, a living person. But the stress is not on the two parts but on the animate living whole. It is not Christian to set body and soul in antithesis. The gospel is not against the body. The ultimate hope for the Christian is the resurrection of the body.

Genesis 2:7 is a definitive passage with regard to the nature of man. We cannot use 1 Thessalonians 5:23 and Hebrews 4:12 to overthrow Genesis 2:7.

There are certain things we need to remember about the body. The body is not evil in itself. Yet it is affected by sin and it is not yet redeemed (Romans 8:23). The body is used by sin, but we are risen with Christ, and so the body is stripped of its power to 'enslave' us to sin. We are to put our bodies at the disposal of God (Romans 6:15–23; 12:1–2). One day our bodies will be raised by Jesus. While we are alive we stress the unity of our person, not its parts. At death the person disintegrates into parts. Meanwhile we *'glorify God in our bodies'* (1 Corinthians 6:19–20).

# Chapter 9

## Paradise

(Genesis 2:8–25)

God puts humankind in an area called Eden, in which is a garden. The story tells us what man and woman were meant to be, and what mankind lost, **and what God wants to give us back in Jesus**.

God plants a garden in the east, in an area east of Israel. In the picture-story of Genesis it was a beautiful place, well-watered and fruitful, a lovely place with pleasant tall trees (see Ezekiel 31:9, 16, 18), among which is a tree called 'the tree of life' (Genesis 2:9). Verse 10 tells us of a river which began in Eden and flowed into the garden. The one river went into the garden then divided into four, and the four became the sources of four great rivers flowing out of the garden into the wider world beyond Eden.

The name 'Eden' means 'delight' or 'place of delightfulness'. Psalm 36:8 uses the word when it refers to the *'river of your delights'*.

We must not try to work out the geography of the garden of Eden. The story deals with real facts but it is told in a very picture-book fashion. Its teaching is more important than its geography.

The garden is a place of great pleasantness. The Greek word *'paradeisos'* which means 'garden' was used later on, and the word 'paradise' came into many of the world's languages. The garden was 'paradise', a special garden of great beauty and in which there was purity and innocence. The rivers which flowed in it and from it give us a picture of life and fertility. Much vegetation grows alongside rivers. The rivers have names (2:11–14). They cannot be identified with four known rivers. Tigris and Euphrates were the names of the two largest rivers in the ancient Near East. The writer uses their names because it gives us the impression of large and mighty rivers. Actually the rivers Tigris and Euphrates do not come from one source, but the writer uses their names for two of the rivers that went out of Eden. The other two names (Pishon and Gihon) are invented names. 'Pishon' comes from a Hebrew word meaning to 'spring up'. 'Gihon' comes from a word meaning to 'bubble up' or to 'burst out'. The names give the impression of lively springs, welling up to give life (see John 4:14 for a parallel).

The rivers water enormous countries. Cush (later used for what we now call Ethiopia and Sudan) and Assyria were watered by these rivers. The writer is still using picture-language, using the names of well-known spacious countries from later times.

The land in which the garden was to be found is described as being rich in valuable metals and minerals.

The picture of the 'garden of Eden' gives us an idea of what God wants for humankind. God wants man to be in a place of abundant provision. When man was right with God he was amazingly and abundantly supplied.

There are some things here that God likes, and that are part of His intention for man.

1. **God likes beauty and desires beauty for the human race**. The garden in Eden was a very beautiful place. It was pleasing to look at (2:9). Christians ought to like beauty and ought to help make this world a beautiful place.

Heaven will be beautiful. The new heavens and new earth of our final glory will be a very beautiful place.

2. **God likes material provision and desires abundance for the human race**. The garden in Eden was richly provided for. There was plenty of food (2:9), there was water, there was gold and there were minerals. *'From every tree you may freely eat'*, said God (2:16). God wants us to be abundantly provided for. Adequate provision is good and right. Sin in the human race has led to poverty. I have no interest in greedy religion, or with people whose motive in church-going is wealth. Provision comes to us as a side-effect of godly living. And there are no rules about guaranteed wealth for the Christian – as the story of Job makes plain. Yet long-term godliness in a people produces prosperity. In the resurrection paradise will be restored; abundance will come to us once again. Meanwhile, whatever our calling is, it is God's will that its needs should be abundantly met.

3. **God likes spiritual liveliness**. In the garden was a *'tree of life'* (2:9). Man was to eat from it and stay alive for ever (see 3:22). There was no natural immortality for men and women. Immortality came to him by his staying obedient to God. But God's intention was that man would stay alive with a God-given liveliness and enjoy fellowship with God (see 3:8) forever. You could say that man and woman were created with a kind of 'eternal life' already.

4. **God likes psychological satisfaction**. Man had a sense of purpose when he was in God's garden. He had work to do for God (2:15). It was happy work, easy work, and would have given him great satisfaction. Genesis 3:17 tells us of how this went wrong, but man was intended to have employment and a sense of worth and of purpose.

5. **God likes companionship** (Genesis 2:18–25). Man was not intended to be alone. At first there was something missing in him. Man is a social creature. He is made

to enjoy other people. God desires friendship and satisfying companionship for the human race. Man tried to get companionship from the animals, but eventually something greater was given him. The human race became man and woman. Man and woman need each other, both one-by-one and community-by-community. Man was made to be a social creature, and not an isolated individual.

This was God's intent. Men and women have lost these blessings, but all of them are given back to us in Jesus.

# Chapter 10

## Innocence Tested

(Genesis 2:16–17)

Humankind was not 'neutral' in the garden of Eden, half-way between righteousness and sin so that he could have gone in either direction. No! In paradise man was righteous. God creates nothing evil. Mankind was made in the image of God, in righteousness and purity.

But his righteousness was untested. The human race was under test as to whether it would maintain the righteousness that God had given it at creation. They were innocent but not confirmed in steadfast righteousness. Adam was told to be obedient (2:16, 17). No other alternative was put before him. Yet there was the possibility that he would disobey. If he sinned by eating from the tree of the knowledge of good and evil, he would come under judgement.

Adam was the head of the human race. He is a representative and agent for the entire human race. The very name means 'man'. In Genesis we read first of 'the man', 'the adam'. Then the word becomes a name, Adam. What happens to Adam happens to 'man'. The first time the word is a name could be Genesis 3:17 or 3:21. It is absolutely certain it is a name as in Genesis 4:25. All mankind is 'in' Adam (see 1 Corinthians 15:21; Romans 5:12–21). The entire human race was involved when Adam sinned. Humankind fell when the most perfect specimen of human righteousness could not maintain his righteousness. What happened to Adam showed what would have happened to any one of us.

God's way of salvation works similarly. In Christ we are restored. Just as Adam represented us, Christ represented us. Christ lived a godly life for us. Christ bore our sins for us.

The tree of the knowledge of good and evil was given that name because man is under test. He will experience good if he obeys the command. He will experience evil if he disobeys the command.

The first reference to any kind of punishment in the Bible is in Genesis 2:17 where Adam is told not to eat of the fruit of the tree of the knowledge of good and evil. *'In the day that you eat of it you shall die'*. From the very beginning of the Bible, the wages of sin is death.

It is not simply the physical termination of earthly life. Adam lived for 930 years! It was not the loss of immortality. Immortality would have been given to Adam via the tree of life if he had been obedient. 'Immortality' was something over and above what he had by virtue of creation (see 3:24). Genesis 2:17 gives the impression that 'death' would come upon Adam immediately if he sinned.

(i) It consists of a **ruined relationship with God**. After his sin the man became full of fear towards God (3:8–10). From this point on humankind will each one be born with a damaged relationship to God. He is born in spiritual death.

(ii) It involves a **ruined relationship with human beings**. After his sin the man who had once delighted in the woman (2:23) now blames her and criticizes her (3:12). This also is immediately seen in what follows the story of man's fall. In the next incident murder comes into the human race. Brother rises up against brother (Genesis 4:8).

As the story of the human race goes on we see progressive decline. Polygamy enters the human race at Genesis 4:19. Murder becomes a matter of pride in the life of Lamech (Genesis 4:23–24).

(iii) It involves a **ruined relationship towards God's creation**. The creation that was originally given to him now will not be so responsive to him. The ground is cursed (3:17). Hardship and toil come into man's labour (3:17). 'Thorns and thistles' come into his environment (3:18). This cursed relationship to physical territory is made even greater in the story of Cain, where he is *'cursed away from the ground'*. He will not have a piece of territory to call his own, and will become a wanderer.

(iv) It involves **vulnerability to the harassment of the serpent**. After Adam's sin a permanent enmity between two human 'seeds' will continue in the human race (3:15). Genesis 6:1–8 is a mysterious passage but it is most likely to be interpreted that as the human race deteriorated it became increasingly vulnerable to evil powers. Genesis 6:1–8 records a grotesque sin, one that no longer can be committed, and one that brought the destruction of the human race in God's judgement, the flood.

(v) It involves **subjection to physical decay and physical death**. Eventually the creative event of Genesis 2:7 will be reversed in Adam's life and he will *'go back to the dust'* (3:19). The point is underlined in Genesis chapter 5, where of each generation it is said *'And he died'*.

(vi) This death also involved **removal from the presence of God**, a change of location. He was no longer allowed in God's paradise. The way for his entry into the presence of God was barred (3:22–24).

When humankind is said to be *'dead in trespasses and sins'*, the thought is wider than physical death in the way the word is ordinarily used. It involves being ruled by Satan (Ephesians 2:2), being under God's wrath and without personal contact with Him (Ephesians 2:3). Being without the life of God. 'Death' in the rest of the Bible is more than simply physical cessation of earthly existence.

Does 'death' in Genesis 2:17 look beyond the grave? Actually there is no discussion of anything 'beyond the grave' in Genesis itself. When the rest of the Bible reveals that the 'death' which comes through sin goes even beyond the grave it is **developing** Genesis 2. In doing so it extends the text of Genesis 2:17. Genesis 2:17 itself does not say anything of what this 'death' might involve **after** Adam has died. Its horizon is earthly. The rest of the Bible will go further.

Revelation 2:7 lets us know that our ultimate heaven will be like the garden of Eden – only there will be more and it will be greater! The 'garden of Eden' will be restored in some way, and God's people will be brought into paradise. Our ultimate glory will be a garden and a city (Revelation 21:2). In the pictures of the other end of the Bible, there is a fountain of life, and the water of life (Revelation 22:1). The curse of the fall will be abolished. We have a fortaste of it even now. *'There is a river whose streams shall make glad the city of God'* (Psalm 46:4). Heaven is anticipated in the church. The church of Jesus Christ is like a temple and the river of life flows through it, to be experienced in different degrees at different times (Ezekiel 47:1–12). Paradise is restored by Christ. It is enjoyed now through Jesus, but ultimately it will be enjoyed in full measure in the new heavens and new earth.

# Chapter 11

## Man and Woman

(Genesis 2:18–25)

Man was not intended to be alone, but is to be a social creature. No one should be an isolated individual.

1. **Man is incomplete without woman**. After the repeated statements in Genesis 1 that *'it was good'*, Genesis 2:18 comes as a surprise. *'It was **not** good that the man should be alone'*. It was not that God had created something evil, but at one point in the sixth 'day' the work was not yet finished. The man was not designed to be a solitary individual; womankind was missing.

I believe this statement partly means that man was – generally speaking – made for marriage. For most men it is true to say that they need womanly companionship. But I also believe that this statement has implications corporately. The sexes should not be segregated too much. All-male company has something missing from it. The opposite is true also. When women get together and there is no male touch about their fellowship there is something missing. The two sexes need each other. All-male groups and all-female groups always seem to have a certain dimension lacking. At more than one level they need each other. Adam was painfully incomplete at this stage of his story (as the deep cry of 2:23 suggests). He was radically and seriously deficient without a wife.

2. The opposite is true. **Womankind is seriously incomplete without man**. In the story of Genesis 2 they are an original unity separated out into a duality (Eve came from Adam's rib). The two sexes were originally one; and they 'click' when they are together again. Woman is incomplete unless she is alongside him. Equally only she can meet Adam's deficiency at this point.

3. **There is significance in the order of events**. Man has been given work to do (2:15). When he was given the task of ruling over the earth, he was alone. *'Man is not from woman, but woman is from man'* (1 Corinthians 11:8). Womankind came in alongside mankind, as an equal partner to help him in the work that he was given to do. There is both equality and leadership here. There is leadership since man was given the task to do, at a point when no woman was present. There is also equality, since the woman is as much in the image of God as the man (see 1:26) and can contribute to the partnership as much as the man. Yet in the order of events man was the 'chairman' in the teamwork between man and woman. There may be exceptions to the rule – but they are exceptions. The sequence of events is important. *'Adam was formed first'*, says Paul, *'then Eve'* (1 Timothy 2:13). It is for this reason that women are not given supreme authority – generally speaking. And it is for this reason that the man is 'head' within marriage (Ephesians 5:22–24). Man's headship is a matter of function, of 'chairmanship' within a team. It has nothing to do with superiority or inferiority. Men and women are equals, but within the equality there is a 'chairman'. He is not 'superior', but in the relationship between the sexes **without** his being superior in himself he has been placed as overseer, or (as I like to put it) 'chairman'. In a committee the 'chairman' may not be the cleverest person around, but for the sake of order he takes the lead.

This is the background to the biblical approach to marriage.

**Marriage is normal and for most people it is needful**. Adam is deficient when he is alone. He needs *'a helper corresponding to him'* (2:18). God invites Adam to study the animals (2:19). Adam's giving names to the animals means that he is studying their nature. Names in the ancient world were descriptions. It is as if Adam is looking to see whether any animal can be an adequate companion for him. But the result is: there was no helper corresponding to him (2:20). Man is not good alone, but animal-companionship is not enough to meet the need.

Marriage is normal and generally necessary. He who finds a wife *'obtains favour from the Lord'* (Proverbs 18:22; see also Proverbs 5:18; 19:22; Proverbs 3l:10–31; Ecclesiastes 9:9; 1 Timothy 4:1–3; 5:14; Hebrews 13:4). In Matthew 19:3–12 Jesus mentions the exceptions to the rule. The disciples raise the possibility that perhaps it is best to stay single. Jesus says only three types of people can accept this. There are (i) those who have no inclination for marriage (*'eunuchs ... from their mother's womb'*); (ii) there are those who are incapable of marriage (*'eunuch ... made eunuchs by men'*); and (iii) there are those who have the gift of singleness and they use that gift for God (*'eunuchs for the kingdom of heaven'*). But Jesus is listing exceptions! Most people are not 'eunuchs' at all!

The early church tended to go astray at this point. Men like Augustine, Jerome and Tertullian, scholars in the early church, had a false view of marriage. It arose from ideas that they inherited from Greek philosophy. So they were all hostile to marriage and sexuality. The early church started 'monasteries' where people vowed not to get married. Tertullian told his wife that if he died she should not remarry. It would be unspiritual, he thought! Then the idea came into the church that preachers should not get married – the celibacy of the clergy! It was all entirely unscriptural. *'Forbidding to marry'* is a *'doctrine of demons'* (see 1 Timothy 4:1–3). *'It is not good for the man to be alone'*.

# Chapter 12

## Marriage

### (Genesis 2:18–25)

1. As I was saying, **marriage is normal and for most people it is needful**. When the woman is brought to the man, he gives a cry of joy. *'This – now – at last'* – he has been waiting for this! – *'is bones of my bones and flesh of my flesh'*. After looking at the animals he says *'At last there is something that corresponds to what I really want'*.

We note that it is not another man that is made (2:23)! The man needed a woman. Unfallen Adam was not homosexual.

1 Corinthians chapter 7 is sometimes thought to point in a different direction. 'Surely Paul is downgrading marriage', it is sometimes said. No. 1 Corinthians 7 must be interpreted in the light of verse 26. There was some 'present distress' in Corinth. Paul is saying, 'In the light of what is happening, this is not the time to be getting married – although you can if you want...'. Notice the difference between 1 Corinthians 7:39–40 and 1 Timothy 5:14. The former is Paul's advice for a stressful situation; the latter is Paul's normal advice in harmony with Genesis and the original gift of marriage to the human race. Marriage is normal and for most people it is needful.

2. **Marriage was ordained by God**. Genesis 2:24 looks to something laid down by God. Marriage is not a matter of

human arrangement or contract. It is not a matter of random evolution.

3. **Marriage is a gift of God's grace**. God caused Adam to fall into a deep sleep while he prepared Eve. As elsewhere in the Bible (see Genesis 15:12) this is a way of stressing God's grace. Adam had nothing at all to do with getting this gift from God. He was asleep at the time. He was totally passive, supernaturally asleep. We are married by grace as well as saved by grace! Eve was a new creation (2:21), brought to the man wholly and exclusively by God (2:22).

4. **We notice the tenderness of the relationship**. It was a cause of great joy to Adam (2:23). It was an intimate relationship, and a pure relationship (2:25). Matthew Henry made a famous comment on this passage: Eve was 'not made out of his head to rule over him, nor out of his feet to be trampled on by him, but out of his side to be equal with him, under his arm to be protected, and near his heart to be beloved.' Eve was made from Adam's rib. Since then man is a bit missing without woman; woman is away from her right place without man.

1 Corinthians 11:7–9 argues for male leadership from Genesis 2:21–22. The woman was brought in to help in a task given to man (2:20). In this, woman is the glory of man. 1 Timothy 2:13–14 makes a similar point.

5. **Marriage is for mankind generally, not for redeemed man exclusively**. It is not a 'sacrament' but a 'creation ordinance'. It is not part of salvation but attached to creation. It is part of God's **general** kindness not part of His **saving** grace. It is not like (for example) water-baptism. Water-baptism is for the church; it is for the saved. You should be saved before you are baptised, but people who are unsaved may nevertheless be truly married. A pagan who gets converted should be baptised, but a pagan who is married does not have to be 'married in church' to be truly

married. People who are not Christians at all may be truly married.

6. **The marriage God envisages is monogamous**. 'They two' are mentioned in Genesis 2:25. Polygamy came in only after man sinned. It was part of the decay of the human race (Genesis 4:19). Lamech, the first polygamist, was an ungodly man (4:23).

7. **Marriage is designed to create independent families** (2:24). An adult child starts a new family. A man leaves father and mother. The 'family' in Genesis 2 is more a small family than an extended family. And the new family has priority over the old family. One's spouse has priority over one's in-laws. The ceremony of 'giving away' the bride is quite meaningful.

8. **Marriage is a public event**. It is not just a secret sexual relationship. It is an open and public and socially recognised commitment of a man and a woman to each other.

9. **Marriage is meant to be permanent**. The man cleaves to his wife. This implies faithfulness, permanence, loyalty, responsibility on the part of the man (for **he** is responsible for the cleaving). It involves *'nourishing and cherishing'* (Ephesians 5:29)

10. **Marriage sets up a 'one flesh' relationship**. This is a very mysterious matter. Paul called it a great mystery (Ephesians 5:31). When a man and a woman are joined together in marriage it sets up a mysterious union of the personality. They are two and yet one at the same time. This is why a sexual relationship is such a powerful thing (see 1 Corinthians 6:16 for the way Paul uses this fact). There comes into being a bond of common interests, pursuits, motivations. This is why it is good for one's partner to be a person of compatible outlook and interests. It calls for wisdom in getting married.

11. **It is notable that marriage is complete without children**. There is no mention of children in Genesis 2.

The marriage is a complete marriage whether there are children or not! This is why it is a mistake to end a marriage because there are no children (as happens in many parts of the world). This means that contraception and birth control are perfectly acceptable for the Christian. A sexual relation is **not** simply for the purpose of having children. The marriage is complete even without children, and the 'one flesh' relationship has significance **other than** its purpose to secure the birth of children.

# *Chapter 13*

# The Snake

## (Genesis 3:1)

Genesis 3 is one of the great chapters of the Bible. It gives
us in picture-style part of an answer to the question: where
did sin come from? It is a story which puts to us very
simply an account of the historical fall of the human race
into sin and into sinfulness. It is a picture-answer to the
question: how does the human race come to need salvation? By 'picture-answer' I mean that it relates a historical
event but it uses a parabolic style to do so. In Genesis 3 a
snake talks, a tree determines the destiny of the human
race, God walks in a garden, another tree can keep
humankind alive for ever. Genesis 1–11 is history written
in a child-like parabolic style. I emphasize both parts of
the sentence. It is history. And it is history **written in a
child-like parabolic style**. Snakes don't talk, and we know
from the New Testament that the snake of Genesis 3 is
parabolic. In the story it really is a snake. Genesis 3:1 says
*'Now the snake was more cunning than any **animal of the
countryside** ... '*. It is an *'animal of the countryside'* that is
mentioned. Yet the picture as a whole refers to something
else. In the book of Revelation the snake is Satan! Satan is
not mentioned directly in the book of Genesis. We are
being told about a real piece of human history but it is
being told parabolically. It refers to historical figures.

Adam is referred to as a historical figure in Luke 3:38.
Genesis 5:3; 1 Chronicles 1:1; 1 Corinthians 15:22. Paul
refers to this incident as a historical event in Romans 5:16,
17. It refers to **one** event, and to the **one** sin of the **one** man.
It is comparable to the **one** act of obedience of the **one**
man Jesus. 1 Timothy 2:13, 14 and John 8:44 similarly
refer to the story of Genesis 3 in a way that implies it is
historical.

In some ways Genesis 3 is like 2 Samuel 12:1–4 where a
real event was being retold parabolically. Yet there is a
difference, for we have no knowledge of the event **behind**
Genesis 3 (unlike the case of 2 Samuel), and we can only
think of the fall of man in terms of the story God has
given us.

1. **Sin began from outside of the human race**. There was
something evil in God's world **before** Eve sinned and
**before** Adam followed her example. This means that sin
is not an essential ingredient in human nature. Sin did
not originate from men and women. It was there even
earlier.

Genesis 3 begins: *'Now the snake was more cunning than
any of the animals of the countryside which Yahweh God
had made. And it said to the woman, "Did God really say
you may not eat from any of the trees of the garden?"'* (3:1).

The word here should be translated 'snake' not 'serpent'.
The English word 'serpent' tends to refer to a mythological
creature, but the word here is a quite ordinary word for an
animal.

The snake is not just a reference to temptations within
us. Nor should the story be taken so literally as to teach
that the fall of man came by a demon-possessed animal.
(This view seems not to take the **parabolic** aspect of the
snake with the seriousness it deserves. The matter-of-fact-
ness of the talking snake is against it; so it is the New
Testament which does not take the snake as a literal snake.)

The main point is that sin is not an essential ingredient in human nature. We are confronted with a talking snake who hates God and beguiles Eve into sin. He is cursed by God. The snake is an animal, yet the Christian knows it refers parabolically to Satan (see Romans 16:20). The word 'devil' is not used. In Genesis 3:15 the snake's head is to be crushed. This refers parabolically to the work of Jesus. Again the parabolic ingredient is obvious. Salvation is not literally the crushing of an animal. The style of language is highly pictorial. It is like the language used to describe heaven in the book of Revelation, where we have the pearly gates of the new Jerusalem (Revelation 21:21), and streets which are made of gold (Revelation 21:21). It is picture language being used in an imaginative way to speak of what is a real event.

There is an evil power in this world. Man was not made sinful. He was not created as a sinner. From outside of his own personality, there comes a being who drags him down into sin. Later parts of the Bible fill out the details. The snake is identified as the devil ('slanderer'), or is called Satan ('adversary'), a being who is like a lion in his ability to inspire fear, and like a snake in his camouflage and deceit.

It is encouraging to know that sinfulness is no part of man's original nature. If we were sinless before, we shall be sinless again, when God's salvation is complete in final glory.

**The devil is real**. It is important to be balanced when thinking about Satan. Some people are so 'scientific' they do not recognize the reality of Satan's existence. Others are so preoccupied with Satan they talk about him day and night. The Bible – which is the model of 'balance' – tells us something about Satan but it is not excessively full of talk about Satan. One can read whole books of the Bible and find Satan not mentioned at all. We must be careful not to get morbid and develop an interest only in 'weird' subjects. We must not get too interested in Satan, but there is no doubt that the devil is real.

# Chapter 14

# The Devil and His Ways

(Genesis 3:1)

2. Consider **the character of the devil**. Although we must not be too interested in him, it is good to know what he is like.

**The devil is powerful**. He is bold. The snake is not afraid to approach Eve and attack God's perfect creation. Satan has power – although his power is less than God's and is under God's control. He has access to us. He can tempt. He has access to the world (see 1 John 5:19; John 12:31; 14:30; 2 Corinthians 4:4; 1 Peter 5:8; Ephesians 2:2).

**The devil is characterised by wickedness**. He has a hatred of God. He hates God's truth, and he hates God's creation. Nowadays he hates God's church. The devil's habit is to seek to spoil everything God does. He wants to ruin the human race, and he seeks to do so by enticing men and women to sin. He is not interested in us personally; he is only interested in ruining God's work. He attacks man not animals or angels. He is not concerned about attacking physical creation, except in order to get at man.

**The devil is characterised by deceit**. He disguises himself and can appear as an angel of light (2 Corinthians 11:13, 14). It is generally difficult to see a snake when it is in its own environment. The snake is a master of camouflage. So the snake comes to Eve. It is pleasant, affable, chatty, seemingly concerned about Eve's welfare.

**The devil is resistible**. This is one piece of good news about him. He is resistible! Resist the devil and he will flee from you.

We might ask 'Where does the devil come from?' We do not know exactly. We can be sure God did not create any wicked creature, and we can be sure that there is nothing in this world that God did not create. So it must mean that the devil was created good but became evil.

Sometimes Ezekiel 28:11–19 is thought to be about Satan. Strictly it is about the king of Tyre, but perhaps it is too extravagant to be just about the king of Tyre. This wicked king is described as being perfect (Ezekiel 28:12), an inhabitant of Eden (Ezekiel 28:13), a cherub (Ezekiel 28:14). He fell through pride (Ezekiel 28:17). Some think this is a shadow of how Satan fell. They may be right (see Isaiah 14:12–13, for a similar passage; and 1 Timothy 3:6; John 8:44; Revelation 12:4, 7).

3. **The snake attacks the man and the woman at their weakest point**. *'The snake was more cunning ... It said to the woman ... '*. God had created man and had given him a task in the garden of God. The woman was created second and she came in to be a help corresponding to him. She was above the animals. No equal companion had been found for the man among the animals. She was a help 'corresponding to' him, equally in the image of God, taken from his rib and therefore made of the same stuff as the man. The snake speaks to her alone. Detached from the man she is out of her true position.

He attacks Eve not Adam (see 2 Corinthians 11:3; 1 Timothy 2:12, 13). Since Adam was Eve's head, Satan is approaching the couple via the one with less authority in this particular matter. I do not mean that a woman always has less authority than a man in dealing with Satan; I only mean that she is in a weaker position if in a crisis she acts without regard to her relationship with her husband. I am not being anti-feminist. Previous eras of human history have often treated women with tyranny, and I would not want to give such wickedness any support. Yet there is no doubt that Satan got Eve to function independently of Adam, and in doing that he was manoeuvring Eve into a position where she was at her weakest. Are men wiser than women? No, not at all! But if a woman steps out of her calling from God, she **becomes** vulnerable. And certainly there is no difficulty in interpreting Paul's words when he says *'it was the woman who was deceived'* (1 Timothy 2:14).

4. **The snake attacks God's Word**. His antagonism concentrates on opposition to God's Word. Here in Genesis 3 he used **doubt** (*'Did God really say...?'*). And he used **perversion of God's Word**, because he suggests Eve may not eat from any tree, but God gave permission to eat from every tree except one – Genesis 2:16–17! And he uses **denial** (*'You will not surely die'*). The Word of God is Satan's great foe. He loves to induce doubt, perversion and denial of the truth of God. This is precisely the way he attacked Jesus. Once again, when he attacked 'the last Adam', our Lord Jesus, he wanted to cause doubt (*'If you are the Son of God...'*, Luke 4:3). Again he perverted God's Word (*'Throw yourself down ... for it is written...'*, Luke 4:9, 10). He used deceit (*'All this authority I will give you ... this has been delivered to me...'*, Luke 4:6).

This is precisely the way Satan will attack the churches. He will draw our attention away from God's written Word. In the modern world Satan has tried to suggest that human reason is adequate to find out the truth. Satan has persuaded large numbers to look to their own ability to heal the world's burdens and agonies. He persuades the churches to neglect God's Word and turn to things more 'exciting'. He spreads the idea that somehow God's Word is not comprehensible, that 'doctrine' is not important, that we can find our own way and work out, without God's Word, how God is leading us. And so the churches are left wanting to know the voice of the Spirit but having no written Word to check whether what claims to be from the Holy Spirit really is from the Holy Spirit. Others try their management techniques and their clever business methods. But it is all of little or no value in the church; the church does not operate in that way. Satan's aim is to rob us of the guidance of God's voice. The way to resist him is to ignore his devices and go back to listening to God's voice coming to us, mainly through Scripture, and always checked by Scripture. Only when we can say *'It is written!'* with authority will we be able to defeat him and strengthen God's kingdom.

# Chapter 15

## Deceit and Defeat

(Genesis 3:2–5)

Satan loves to slander God, and attacks God's reliability, His faithfulness (3:4), His goodness (3:1b). He likes to suggest that God is harsh and restrictive. In point of fact, it is sin and Satan which are harsh towards us.

The story continues: *'And the woman said to the snake, "We may eat from the fruit of the trees of the garden (3:2), but from the fruit of the tree which is in the middle of the garden God has said 'You shall not eat from it, nor shall you touch it, or you will die'"* (3:3). *And the snake said to the woman, "You will certainly not die (3:4). For God knows that as soon as you eat from it your eyes will be opened, and you will be like God, knowing what is good and evil"'* (3:5).

Consider **the aims of the devil** (Genesis 3:1–6). He wants to insinuate an anti-God approach to life. In every area he wants to get people away from God, and he wants to take over as though he were God himself.

He wants to get us away from God **as the source of knowledge**. Here he is drawing Eve away from God as the one who knows everything that there is to know. He speaks as if he knows more than God. He wants to get Eve away from God's Word as a source of knowledge, and replaces God's revelation by making himself the source of knowledge.

He wants to get us away from God **as the source of authority**. He acts as if he has a right to speak, and to lay down what is right and what is wrong. He dismisses God as having any authority at all, and yet acts with supreme confidence in himself.

He wants to get us away from God **as the guide to conduct**. He suggests a different style of living for Eve, compared to what God has said.

He wants to get us away from God **as the one who controls our destiny**. If Eve eats of the tree which is in the middle of the garden God has said what her destiny will be. *'You shall surely die'*. Satan instead says *'You shall not die'*. God claims to be in control of our destiny and to have the ability to say what will happen to us. Satan wants to get us away from God as the controller of our destiny and he suggests that he knows what our destiny will be and it is other than what God has said.

He wants to get us away from God **as the source of pleasure**. He suggests that a great life is available to us as we follow him. Satan suggests to Eve, and to men and women today, that the pleasurable life is the life that neglects and turns away from God. Actually the Bible claims that at God's right hand there are *'pleasures for evermore'*. We tend to think that the godly life is somehow narrow and restrictive. The devil suggests to us that there is great pleasure if we follow our own way – which in fact is following his way, for he deceives us. He says to us *'All things will I give you if . . . '* and seeks to get us to believe that the life of joy and happiness is the life that shuns God.

He wants to get us away from God **as the one we worship**. He suggests that Adam and Eve will become like gods if they follow him. The idea is that God will no longer be any kind of supreme King of the universe. They will become their own gods. God will no longer have to be worshipped as God. Man will be his own god.

Satan still lies, and he still tells the same lies. He flatters, without our even knowing that it is his voice that we are hearing. Satan is always plausible. He uses rising pressure and comes to us at our weakest point. He wants to control our minds, our worship, our conduct, our experience. He wants to keep us laden with guilt. He wants to hold us in darkness.

Consider next **the way of defeat**. How did Satan succeed in getting Eve to sin?

1. **She got talking to the snake**. But why should she do that? It is a great mistake to have any kind of discussion with Satan. Why should she engage in a dialogue? She replies to him, but there was no need for her to do so. This talking snake that rises up against God has no right to an answer. It is not a genuine sympathizer with Eve. It is a mistake to think we have to answer our enemies all the time. It is not necessary. And it leads to Eve's accepting the snake at face value. She receives the snake's way of presenting itself.

2. **She accepted his perverted use of God's Word, and even perverted it herself**. She said *'We may eat from the fruit of the trees of the garden...'*. She felt she had to defend God! Then she said *'...but from the fruit of the tree which is in the middle of the garden God has said "You shall not eat from it, nor shall you touch it..."'*. No! God did not say anything about not touching it. Eve had been persuaded to think of God as harsh. Now she is the one perverting God's Word.

3. **She keeps listening**. As the snake continues, *'You will certainly not die ... your eyes will be opened ... you will be like God...'*, Eve was still listening! Satan wants to keep us listening to him. He progresses from one level of deceit to another and we are changed not from one degree of glory to another (see 2 Corinthians 3:18), but into willingness to sin and on to yet greater willingness to sin.

## *Chapter 16*

# The Devil's Lines of Attack

### (Genesis 3:6)

Consider the devil's **avenues of attack**. Eve was well on the way to falling when she queried God and listened to the snake. She was already misrepresenting God's Word (3:3b). Already she was listening to Satan and querying God's power. Already she has fallen in her mind and in her spirit although she had not done anything yet. Genesis 3:6 deals with how the sin comes out in the deed.

James 1:14 says *'Each person is tempted and put to the test when he is attracted and enticed by that person's own desire.* (verse 15) *Then the desire conceives and gives birth to sin, and when sin is full-grown it gives birth to death'*. These stages are visible in the story of Eve's fall. She looks at the tree, prompted by the snake. She is enticed by the attractiveness of the fruit and is lured by her desires. Then desire gets a hold, and it gives birth to the sin. The result is disaster, spiritual death. Soon she will be driven out of paradise, and away from God.

Sin uses three avenues. First there is **the lust of the flesh**. One channel by means of which sin pulls at us is our very physical frame. *'When the woman saw that the tree was good for food, and that it was a delight to the eyes, and that the tree was to be desired to make one wise, she took of its* *fruit and ate; and she also gave some to her husband, who was with her, and he ate'* (3:6).

The desire for food was part of what drew Eve into sin. The body exercises a pull on us and sin can use our various physical appetites. There are various desires of the body, the desire for ease, laziness, appetite, greed for physical pleasure, sexuality. All of these are channels down which we may be drawn into sin. The woman saw the fruit was good for food. It appealed to her hunger, her taste for physical nourishment.

Secondly, there is **the lust of the eyes**. The power of eyesight has an amazing ability to stimulate the desire for sin. It is stronger in this than any other of the body's senses. Eve *'saw that it was good ... and that it was a delight to the eyes ...'*. Our appetite for something sinful will be heightened by our seeing it. There is an added desire that comes by looking, enticements that come through the imagination stirred by something seen. The fruit was *'a delight to the eyes'*. The inclination to sin came to Eve when she saw the fruit. This often happens. Sin often attacks when people notice something. *'As soon as he had seen the ring and the bracelets ...'* (Genesis 24:30), Laban was wondering how he could exploit Abraham's servant. *'I saw a fine robe ... I set my heart on them ... I took them'*, said Achan (Joshua 7:20, 21). David *'saw a woman bathing ...'* (2 Samuel 11:2) and soon his kingdom was almost in ruins. Lot **saw** the enticing riches of the area where Sodom and Gomorrah were to be found (Genesis 13:11–12). When we are in fellowship with the Lord we are to be 'watchful' for the approach of sin. Outside of God we look around and we see many things which stimulate our appetites for sin. We are 'watchful' in a wrong way. If sinless Eve could be pulled down, how much more those who are born sinful.

Thirdly, there is **the pride of life** (the third of the three mentioned in 1 John 2:16). Sin appeals to human vanity. Eve now wanted to be independent of God. She wanted to be independently wise, leading her own life without God. She had a desire to be superior, to 'be wise'.

Soon came the 'conception' of sin. This is when sin deposits itself into our innermost hearts, and we now intensely and blindly want to sin. Sin is more than temptation, and temptation is not sin. Sin takes hold or 'conceives' within us at the point when it is welcomed or cherished. Satan will put thoughts in our mind, but that is not sin. It only becomes sin when we receive his suggestions.

Next comes the birth of sin. Eve acts. She takes the fruit and eats. She did not get the snake to change as she chatted to him, but he got her to sin.

Eve was deceived (see 1 Timothy 2:14), but Adam was not. Adam was appointed to be leader and Eve was to allow him to be the authority in Eden. In refusing this role and acting independently Eve was deceived. If women today refuse their role, they will again be deceived. I am **not** saying that women generally are more able to be deceived, but if they refuse their womanly role, their refusal to accept God's plan for them leads to deception.

Eve was fallen already when she queried God. She had fallen in her mind and spirit already. Verse 6 deals with how the sin comes out in the actual deed of taking from the forbidden fruit.

The same three channels of attack, the desire of the flesh, the desire of the eyes, and the pride of life (see 1 John 2:16) were used again in the temptation of Jesus (Matthew 4:1–11). Satan wanted (i) stones to be made into bread, and (ii) showed Jesus the glory of the world's kingdoms, and (iii) urged Jesus to do something that would bring Him immediate admiration and favour among the people. However the second Adam was victorious where Eve and the first Adam failed. He did not doubt the Word of God (*'Has God really said...?'*) but trusted the Word of God (*'It is written...!'*).

# Chapter 17

## Paradise Lost

### (Genesis 3:6–7)

Eve *'also gave it to her husband with her and he ate'*. Satan used Eve to get Adam to sin. Adam was not deceived (1 Timothy 2:14). He sinned knowingly and wilfully. He deliberately followed her into a forbidden area. She went there having been deceived; he walked into the kingdom of sin with his eyes wide open. The human race did not die through Eve. It was 'in Adam', not 'in Eve' that all die (1 Corinthians 15:22).

Sin brings after it a trail of consequences. They can be seen in the story of what happened to Adam and Eve; and the human race has been living with the repercussions of Adam's sin ever since.

How should Eve have resisted Satan? **She should not have stepped out of her calling and her role**. She should have passed the snake on for Adam to deal with. He was there (*'her husband, who was with her'*, 3:6)! We fall when we try to exercise an authority we do not have. If we act outside of what God is calling us to do we become foolish and we get deceived.

She should have refused Satan's claims. A long discussion was not needed. The people of God give short answers to Satan. *'It is written!' 'Get behind me'*. There is no need for long conversations, nor even long periods of 'binding Satan' – that is not found in Scripture at all! The devil is not reasonable. There is no point in trying to reason with him. If you start discussing matters with Satan or listening to his lies you will have fallen as soon as you start the discussion. Eve **trusted** what Satan said!

How do we resist Satan? Keep in fellowship with Jesus. Temptations lose their power when Jesus is near. Trust in Jesus. Call upon Him in time of attack. He is always near. Be saturated with the truth of God. Be covered with the righteousness of Jesus. Enjoy your relationship with God.

When Satan attacks be ready to trust God's promises. Expect that God will bring you through. Often one verse of Scripture keeps your mind clear. *'It is written...!'* Above all be much in prayer.

Then 'Stand!' Refuse to yield! And God will bring you through. If we resist Satan there is nothing he can do. He runs from us, when he sees that we are resisting him *'in the Lord and in the power of Jesus' might'* (Ephesians 6:10).

We are to do the exact opposite of everything he wants. If Satan's purpose is to get God out of our lives, our purpose is to bring God into every department of our existence. Jesus becomes for us the source of knowledge, the supreme authority, the guide to conduct, the one who holds our destiny in His hands, our greatest joy and pleasure, the only one we worship. In the Lord Jesus Christ we resist Satan at every point. In Jesus we can do it.

However, Adam and Eve fail in all of this. They sin and soon a trail of disaster is upon them.

1. First, **they get what they want but they do not want it**. The snake had promised that if they sinned their eyes would be opened, and that is what happens. *'The eyes of both of them were opened and they knew that they were naked; and they sewed fig leaves, and made for themselves*

*coverings'* (3:7). The tree of the knowledge of good and evil was designed to bring Adam and Eve into a knowledge of sin and holiness. But this knowledge was to come to them **by resisting sin**. The best way to come to an understanding of sin is by resisting it. Jesus knew more about sin than anyone but He never sinned! His knowledge of 'good and evil' came because he resisted sin.

Adam and Eve came into a knowledge of sin by becoming guilty of it. The snake offered them a knowledge of good and evil, and that is what they obtained, but they obtained it in the wrong way. It brought them shame. They got what they wanted but then they found it was not something wonderful that they had received but something that brought guilt.

Often Satan can rouse in us the most intense desire for something, but then when we get it we find we do not want it. One of David's sons intensely wanted Tamar his sister, but the moment he had taken her in a forceful and wicked way he no longer wanted what he had got. The eyes of Adam and Eve were indeed opened (as the snake had said) but only in a way that produced remorse.

This is 'death'. God had told them it would come upon them as soon as they sinned. They had a kind of knowledge of good and evil, but they were now without God. They had wanted independence from God; now they had it. Their eyes were open in a way they had not expected. At the point when Eve was holding a friendly conversation with the snake, she was blind to the consequences of what would happen. We are all quite blind at the height of seductive temptation.

Nakedness was now to them a parable of guilt. Shame and a sense of failure left them feeling exposed. Adam and Eve got what they wanted but then they did not want it. An experience of evil by being in it is terrible. It is better to know the greatness of wickedness by withstanding it.

Thank God for Jesus! We can be so glad that we know about Jesus bearing our sins on the cross, and coming alive to rule in our lives. He forgives our sins and clothes us with the clean clothes of His righteousness.

# Chapter 18

# Running from God

(Genesis 3:8–13)

The sin of Adam and Eve brought a whole chain of consequences into their own lives and into the life of the human race.

2. **They become self-conscious because of their guilt and shame**. They feel their nakedness (3:7). Before they had felt free from self-consciousness, free from any desire to hide. But now they cannot undo what they have done and they feel guilty before God and before each other.

3. **They start making attempts to compensate for their guilt**. They sewed fig-leaves together to make themselves loin-cloths. Having fallen into sin they now take the matter of salvation into their own hands and decide to do what they can to compensate for their sense of guilt and shame. Since they feel so naked and exposed now, they decide to take matters into their own hands by providing a device to save themselves from this sense of exposure.

Sinners like to try to save themselves. They seek for what one could call 'fig-leaf salvation', a salvation of their own providing. It may take the form of religiosity or rigid severity with oneself. People turn to the 'sacraments', baptism and the Lord's Supper, and some want to add more ceremonies and rituals. They feel somehow 'covered' before God if they engage in the observance of rites and ceremonies. Others become legalistic and make rules for themselves, promising God they will do this or that. Many simply become highly moral and respectable and hope that God will accept their feeble attempts at being righteous. Some turn to 'mysticism', trying to find God by experiences and feelings and emotions which they work up within themselves.

It is all 'fig-leaf salvation'; none of it does any good. Salvation has to come from God or there is no salvation at all.

4. **They no longer want fellowship with God**. Despite their attempts to cover their guilt, when God comes seeking to talk with them, as He had done before, they no longer want to meet with Him. *'And they heard the sound of Yahweh God walking in the garden, at the cool time of the day. And the man and his wife hid themselves from the presence of Yahweh God among the trees of the garden'* (3:8). Before God had said anything to them, they wanted to avoid God. Sin produces in us a wrong kind of fear of God. We feel guilty. We feel that punishment is likely to fall on us. The sinner resents God. He may like the idea of God. He may use the word 'god', but when the God of the Bible comes to him, he or she wants to run. The *'natural man'* (as Paul would say, 1 Corinthians 2:14) is an enemy of God.

God comes seeking fellowship, but they no longer want fellowship with God. They now have a bad conscience, and their only reaction when God comes seeking them is to avoid Him.

*'And Yahweh God called to the man, and said to him, "Where are you?"'* (3:9). The language is picture-language. God is pictured as taking human form and as seeking information. The picture language must not be taken too literally. *'And he said, "I heard the sound of you in the garden, and I was afraid, because I was naked, and I hid myself"'* (3:10).

82

Adam wants only to hide. He actually chooses the very gifts of God – the trees – and uses them to conceal himself from God. The human race has been running from God ever since. When we turn to Jesus, only then do we experience the undoing of the calamity that fell upon the human race through Adam.

5. **They now begin shifting blame**. Since they do not want to admit any kind of guilt, and since their attempts at covering themselves have all failed, their next device is to shift the blame elsewhere. *'And He said, "Who told you that you were naked? Have you been eating from the tree concerning which I commanded you not to eat?"'* (3:11). The now feel the scrutiny of God concerning their sin and since they do not want to admit any kind of guilt their remedy is to shift the blame elsewhere. *'And the man said, "That woman you gave to be with me – she gave me the fruit from the tree and I ate it"'* (3:12). They are responding deceitfully to God's questions. Sin is evasive. God asks about the source of their knowledge. It could have come by resisting sin, but God knows that Adam and Eve have sinned. They are evasive. The sinner blames everyone except himself. First the man blames the woman. This is the same one about whom he had said *'This at last, now, is bone of my bones and flesh of my flesh'*; the one he had loved so much and over whom he had been rejoicing, he now blamed for what he had done. He had once been so grateful to God, but now he blames Him, *'You gave her to me'*.

Sin disrupts friendship and companionship. Previously he had joined her in her sin; now it does not seem to worry him if she comes under God's judgement. He has become careless and without compassion for the one he had loved so much.

The woman blames the snake. *'And Yahweh God said to the woman, "What is this that you have done?" And the* woman said, "The snake deceived me, and I ate" ' (3:13). No one blames himself. Yet we cannot use even the devil as the excuse for our sin. We are meant to resist the devil. When we stand before God we shall give an account of ourselves and we shall not be able to point to anyone else, not even the devil.

Men and women have been running from God ever since. Only Jesus can undo what Adam and Eve did.

# Chapter 19

# The Seed of the Woman

(Genesis 3:14–15)

Adam and Eve have been trying to avoid admitting any kind of sin or guilt. They have made clothing from fig-leaves with which to cover themselves. They have put the blame elsewhere and refused to admit frankly what they have done.

The only hope for them is that God Himself should do something about their plight. God did not question Satan in the way that He had questioned Adam and Eve. Satan is beyond redemption. There would be no point in God seeking to bring the snake to repentance. Instead God simply pronounces His verdict upon the snake.

*'And Yahweh God said to the snake, "Because you have done this you are cursed above every living animal of the countryside. You shall go on your belly, and you shall eat dust all the days of your life"'* (3:14). 'The snake' is cursed. Satan is cursed by God. To 'eat dust' is a phrase meaning to be utterly defeated. It is not necessary to think that some change in the shape of the snake takes place. We must not think of a beautiful upright shining serpent which now becomes a snake. Genesis 3:14 is using picture-language. It simply means that the hissing, wriggling, slithering, deceitful, camouflaged, dangerous way that the snake behaves, is a picture of the enemy of God

and his people. The snake was always like that but now his form is to remind us of Satan every time we see a snake. (It is like the rainbow. It was always there, even before Genesis 9:13 but after the flood it became a sign.)

When God turns to the woman He does not curse her. The snake is doomed but the guilty couple are not cursed in quite the same way. The devil is beyond salvation but the woman is not beyond salvation.

God says, *'And I will put enmity between you and the woman, and between your seed and her seed'.*

In Genesis 2:19 men and women were above the animals. Genesis 3:1–7 gave us a picture of a talking animal that hates God and rises above its natural position, wishing to ruin the human race. It is a parable of one who hates God, *'the old serpent, the Devil, Satan'* (Revelation 20:2).

1. **The snake will not be allowed to be 'friendly' to the woman again**. There will be *'enmity between you and the woman'.* Eve will from now on know that the snake is an enemy not a friend.

2. **The snake will have a seed**. This does not refer to evil spirits but to human beings who succumb to Satan and in some sense have him as their spiritual 'father'. (*'You are of your father, the devil ... He was a murderer from the beginning'*, said Jesus, John 8:44.)

3. **The woman will have a seed**. She will be the enemy of the snake and there will be many of her descendants who will also be opposed to the snake, that is, opposed to Satan. The human race will divide into two, those who are on the side of the snake and those who are allied to the woman in her opposition to the snake.

4. **The seed of the woman will crush the snake's head**. *'He shall crush your head, and you shall crush his heel'* (3:15). The Hebrew word here means 'to crush, to batter, to seriously bruise'. When you kill a snake you crush its head.

This is a prophecy that somehow humankind will eventually defeat the snake and the snake's seed.

But how can this be? Perfect Adam, who was in daily fellowship with God, and had never sinned, was able to fall. Now the human race is fallen and is in the grip of guilt, and about to be banished from God's presence. How can the 'seed of the woman' ever hope to defeat the snake who has shown such skill and such power?

The prophecy has a question in it. How can the human race ever hope to defeat Satan if sinless unfallen Adam had not been able to do so? And yet there is a prediction that it will.

Yet another thing ought to be noticed. The word 'seed' is strangely ambiguous. It can refer to a single entity, 'a seed'. It can be a collective word, 'seed' meaning many seeds.

Genesis 3:15 leaves open the possibility that somehow there will be **one** seed who will conquer the snake for the rest of the human race. This is not just a matter of reading something into the text. The text itself leaves us baffled. How can there ever be anything or anyone within the human race that can defeat the snake? The best man there ever was – unfallen Adam – had failed. How can any other human being do better?

It can only mean one thing. Somehow within the human race there will be a Conqueror who will crush the snake. One will come who will undo everything the snake has done. He will banish the guilt, the shame, the nakedness. He will bring back paradise, and the harmony of Eden once again. He will bring men and women back to God so that once again they can have fellowship with Him as Adam and Eve had done.

Genesis 3:15 is the first announcement of the gospel, the first prophecy of Jesus. It was mysterious and obscure, and must have left its original readers tantalized. It left the question: how can the snake be defeated by someone within the human race?

5. **The serpent would crush the heel of the seed of the woman**. Crushing the head is administering a fatal blow. Crushing or bruising the heel is administering a blow from which there can be recovery.

Jesus crushed Satan on the cross. Satan bruised Jesus on the cross. Satan will never recover. He is crushed for ever. Jesus recovered. He was bruised to the point of death, but then rose. Jesus recovered from the cross; Satan will never recover.

# Chapter 20

## Adam's Faith

(Genesis 3:16–20)

The fallenness of the world is being blamed on to man, not on to God. God created man with a certain amount of freedom. Men and women misused that freedom. Why did God give man such freedom in the first place? Perhaps God did not want a robot who was totally controlled. Perhaps after the redeemed section of the human race is fully restored, the universe will be greater than what could have been if man had never fallen. Such matters are pressing into *'the secret things'* (Deuteronomy 29:29). Genesis is recording the immediate results of sin.

1. **Pain entered the world because of sin**. There was no kind of 'evil' pain before Adam's sin. But now there is a change. *'To the woman he said, "I shall greatly multiply your pains in childbirth. In pain you will bear children. Your ambition will be for your husband, but he shall rule over you"'* (3:16). Perhaps some kind of 'good' pain was known before the sin of Adam, the kind of pain that gives us friendly warnings, or that prevents us from doing damage to ourselves. Yet whatever might have been present before the fall, pain is intensified greatly after the sin of Adam. Pain in childbirth is a reminder of the sin of Eve.

2. **Ugliness came into relationships between the sexes.** *'Your ambition will be for your husband'*, said God to the

woman. The relationship between the sexes would be damaged. Now the woman will have 'ambition'. It seems that this word means 'desire to control'. It is the same word used in Genesis 4:7 when God said to Cain *'Sin's ambition is for you'* or *'Sin is ambitious to get you'*. Womanly compliance becomes a desire to change and control the husband.

The husbandly side of the relationship goes wrong also: *'he shall rule over you'*. The woman's role and the man's role both become perverted. The woman tends to want to subtly control the man. The man tends to dominate and tyrannize.

3. **The very ground of the earth was damaged**. God turns next to Adam. *'To Adam he said, "Because you have obeyed the voice of your wife, and have eaten from the tree about which I commanded you, saying 'You shall not eat from it',*
*the land is cursed because of you.*
*In pain you will eat of it*
*all the days of your life* (3:17).
*Thorns and thistles it shall grow for you,*
*and you will eat the plants of the countryside* (3:18).
*By the sweat of your face you shall eat bread,*
*until you return to the ground.*
*For from it you were taken.*
*For you are dust,*
*and to dust you shall return"'* (3:19).

Adam's judgement is the longest. God rebukes Adam's misuse of the role that God had given him (*'Because you have obeyed the voice of your wife...'*) and the sin he had committed (*'...and have eaten from the tree...'*). From now on the land will be affected. Crops will grow only with difficulty and toil. Eden was a good land, well-watered and fertile, but that will cease. Man will be excluded from Eden (see 3:24) and eventually Eden will be withdrawn. There is no longer a 'garden of Eden' on planet earth.

Pain has been mentioned already in connection with Eve, but Adam will experience it also (3:17). Eve will suffer when she is a mother; Adam will suffer when he is a farmer and food-producer. Hardships will enter in; 'thorns and thistles' will make life hard for the farmer. Sin brings ecological disaster.

4. **Work becomes laborious**. Work had been part of paradise (2:15) but now an added note of severity and hardship comes in. Man no longer likes toil. It is not as sweet to him as it was before.

5. **Death grips the human race**. Man experiences spiritual death immediately and because of his fallenness will experience physical death eventually (3:19).

However there is good news as well as bad news. Adam and Eve respond positively to God's judgement upon them. We read: *'Now the man called his wife's name "Eve", because she was the mother of all living'* (3:20). Despite what Adam had done, he accepts God's verdict, and he believes God's promise. God's grace proves to be greater than Adam's sin. Adam calls his wife 'Eve' or *'Chawwah'* (as it is spelt in Hebrew). The name is a word meaning 'She who gives life'. I do not think it means merely that the whole human race will descend from her. That may be true, but I do not think it is the point of the name. Surely it is an expression of faith in the promise of Genesis 3:15.

Eve might well have been called 'mother of all dying'. The entire human race fell under the dominion of death because of the sin of Eve and the following sin of Adam. God has just said so: *'You are dust, and to dust you shall return'*. Eve is the mother of all people but they will all die! Yet Adam names his wife 'She who gives life'. It surely is Adam's way of saying that he believes in what God has promised in Genesis 3:15. The snake has brought death into the world, but through the woman somehow there is going to come in to the human race, One who will crush the snake's head. Death will become life. The fall of man will be reversed. Life for all people will come through the seed of the woman and therefore in a sense through the woman herself. Adam believes it and names his wife: 'She who gives life'. He believes that somehow, through her seed, life will come to the human race.

# *Chapter 21*

## Delayed Glory

(Genesis 3:21–24)

Two things happen through Adam's believing in the promise of Genesis 3:15.

1. First, Adam and Eve receive clothing from God. *'And Yahweh God made garments of skin for Adam and for his wife, and he clothed them'*. In the garden of Eden, nakedness expressed innocence. Consciousness of nakedness expressed shame (Genesis 3:7, 21). From now on it is shameful to be naked in public (see Genesis 9:22, 23).

God's provision of clothes is a way of expressing the fact that when we believe, He clothes us with garments of salvation. We are covered with righteousness; the Christian can say he has the righteousness of Jesus (2 Corinthians 5:21). He has bright clothing; he is full of joy. He has clean clothing because he himself is clean in God (Mark 9:3; Revelation 3:4). He soon will be clothed with the clothing of a glorious resurrection body (2 Corinthians 5:1–2).

We note that the clothing required the death of a substitute. By the death of a sacrifice clothing came from that sacrifice. By the death of God's Son we come to be clothed with the righteousness of God's Son.

2. However there is a second aspect to the matter. **Adam and Eve's salvation is not complete**. They do not get to final glory. One day we shall be 'raised' with 'an imperishable

body', *'raised in glory ... raised in power ... raised a body for the Spirit'* (1 Corinthians 15:42–44) but Adam had not reached that level of glory.

Adam and Eve were not released from the fact that they would die. When we receive salvation it is a salvation in our relationship to God, but we are still *'waiting for ... the redemption of our body'* (Romans 8:23). Adam was brought into **that** position. So he had to be put out of the garden of Eden. He could enjoy a relationship with God, but he could not yet enjoy resurrection-glory. The **physical** sign of God's anger towards sin remains for the moment.

Man had come to a knowledge of good and evil. He had known a taste of good (because he was once sinless); he had a taste of evil (because he was now a sinner). Now God speaks again. *'And Yahweh God said, "Behold the man has become like one of us in knowing good and evil. And now lest he stretch out his hand and also take fruit from the tree of life and so eat it and live for ever ... "* (3:22), *and Yahweh God put him out of the garden of Eden to work the ground from which he had been taken'* (3:23).

Humankind could have lived for ever, not because they were naturally immortal but by eating of the tree of life. Now they are excluded. Man loses eternal life in fellowship with God. He had that originally. He was in fellowship with God, and God and man met with each other in the cool of the day. Life in fellowship with God was due to go on for ever. That is what 'eternal life' is. It is life that goes on for ever, but it is also a special kind of life. It is life in closeness with God. Adam had known that life and should have lived forever without death.

But now as a result of his sin he loses that. He is put out of access to the tree of life.

*'And He thrust the man out, and at the east of the garden of Eden He placed the cherubim and the flaming sword*

*which turned in every direction to guard the way to the tree
of life'* (3:24).

God was reconciled to Adam, but it was still necessary
for Him to express His hatred of sin. Adam's final
salvation, even in the body, has not yet come. God thrust
out the man and the woman, and put cherubim – some
kind of angels – to guard the way so that Adam could not
get back. A flaming sword turned every way to guard the
way. No matter from which direction Adam came he could
not get back to paradise.

All of that happened as the result of the fall. Is there any
way back? There is one note of hope, in Genesis 3:15, of
the entire situation being reversed. The human race will
divide into two. Out of the woman will come a 'seed'.
From that 'seed' will come a Saviour. He will be born as a
human being, as *'the Seed of the woman'*. He will strike a
fatal blow, and undo all that Satan has done.

This release from Satan comes in stages. For many
centuries God prepares the way. Then there comes one
who is not born of a human Father but is the seed of a
woman. He lives the life we should have lived. He died as
we should have died. He has perfect righteousness, perfect
faith. And He makes a perfect way of salvation.

As we believe in Jesus the work of Satan is reversed. If
Satan got us to sin, Jesus gets us to live for God. If the
snake engineered the fall, Jesus brings a restoration. If
the devil put us out of eternal life Jesus brings us back into
eternal life. If Satan's work resulted in our being power-
fully driven out of paradise, Jesus' work will bring us back
and keep us safe for ever. He undoes all that the snake has
done, undoing the guilt of sin, the power of sin, eventually
wiping out even the very presence of sin.

By faith in Him we receive eternal life. It is as if we are
back in the garden of Eden.

# Chapter 22

## The Bible and Early History
### (Genesis 4:1–26)

From about the end of Genesis 4 it is possible to see contacts with the story of our world as it is studied by historians, and to date some of what is happening. At Genesis 4:1 we are apparently at about 13,000 BC.

According to Genesis 1:1–2:3 God created the world including the human race. The 'days' of Genesis 1 are part of the picture-language of the story and are not to be used to give a date to creation. Scientists say that the universe is perhaps 4,000,000,000,000 years old. They also have their ideas about the date of planet earth, and the date of the first man-like creatures, and the date of modern man about 100,000–75,000 years ago, but no dates are given in the Bible.

It seems from the various human remains that have been found, that the modern human race originated in Africa or maybe in the 'fertile crescent' about 100,000–75,000 BC, and then spread out through Africa, Europe and Asia (see Map 1, p. 97).

At about 20,000 BC human beings found their way into the American continent and into Australia (see Map 2, p. 97).

There was only one human race. The whole of humanity is *'of one blood'* (Acts 17:26). Long before 20,000 BC the

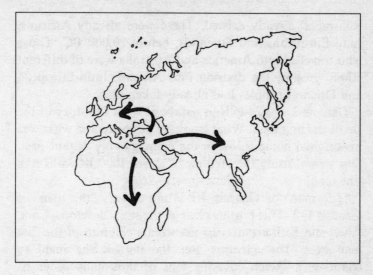

Map 1: *The spread of the human race*

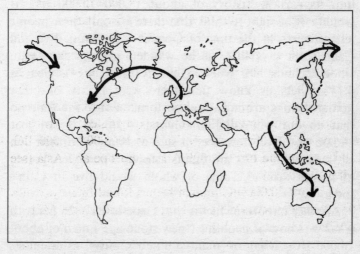

Map 2: *Humans spread into America and Australasia*

'sub-races' already existed. There were already Africans, Indo-Europeans and Orientals, before 20,000 BC. Those who travelled into America and Australia were of different ethnic groups; the division into African, Indo-European and Oriental peoples had already taken place.

Genesis 2:4–3:24 tells in parabolic form the story of the sin of the first man. What language he spoke and what was his original name is lost in the unimaginably distant past. Our writer, using the Hebrew of about 1000 BC calls him 'the man'.

'The man' of Genesis 4:1 is not strictly 'the man' of Genesis 1–3. This is quite clear as the story develops. Cain, Abel, and Seth are not the immediate children of the first man ever. The narrator uses the phrase 'the man' to condense a sketch covering tens of thousands of years. Because of the compressed style of picture-like history, Genesis 4:1 in effect means *Someone in the line of the man and his wife gave birth to a son . . .*.

We are now moving into the Mesopotamian world, and into its earliest history of about 13,000–10,000 BC. It would not be right to think that there are only three people left on earth at the time of Genesis 4:1, Adam, Eve and Cain. Cain says that, as he wanders around the earth, whoever finds him will kill him (Genesis 4:14). Genesis 4:14–15 lets us know that there were plenty of other human beings around. God performs a sign for Cain so that no one will kill him (Genesis 4:15). It is not that 'Adam and Eve' now need a sign to know who their son is! In Genesis 4:17 Cain builds a town. There were plenty of people around, some of whom would live in Cain's town.

Another important fact is that Genesis 4:17–26 fits with what we know of neolithic ('new stone-age') man of about 10,000 BC. 'Modern' man – 'homo sapiens' as scientists call him – goes back at least as far as 50,000 BC and maybe much earlier. If the event of Genesis 1:26–27 is to be dated earlier than 50,000 BC and if Genesis 4:17–26 is at about 10,000 BC then we are leaping over tens of thousands of years in a few verses of Genesis.

The Hebrew word *'adam* (in which ' represents the Hebrew letter *'aleph*) occurs 34 times in Genesis 1–5. It means 'man' or 'humankind'. It stands both for a section of the history of the human race and for different individuals. Twenty-two times [1] *ha'adam* ('the man') is used referring either to 'humanity' (Genesis 1:27) or to an unnamed individual (e.g. 2:7).

The word (without 'the') in 1:26 and 2:7 means 'humanity' or 'a man'. Three times the word is preceded by the Hebrew *lamed* ('to', 'for') and on such occasions the consonantal text cannot distinguish between 'the man' and 'Adam'. But 2:20 probably means 'for a man'; 3:17 could mean 'to Adam'; and 3:21 could mean 'for Adam'. [2]

Actually the first place in the Bible where *'adam* seems to be a name, 'Adam', is Genesis 4:25. Then the word appears apparently as a name in Genesis 5:3, 4, 5. Before that one could often almost translate *'adam* by 'Mr Human Race' or 'Mr Humankind'.

What all this means is that there is a strong suggestion in the text itself that 'Mr Human Race' refers to different people at different times. Scarcely ever is *'adam* a name. When it is a name it has the 'feel' of 'Mr Human Race'. **There is an obvious leap of time between Genesis 1–3 and Genesis 4:1**. So 'Mr Human Race' is not always the same person. In Genesis 5:1 the word occurs twice. It is generally first translated 'Adam' and then translated 'man' – but it is the same word.

Genesis 1–4 is highly compressed and leaps over thousands of years. This is why Genesis 4:14–15 can talk as if there were thousands of people around, and Cain can be the builder of a town (4:17). Cain, Abel and Seth were sons of 'the man' but they were not one generation after 'the man' of Genesis 1–3. The people of the Americas and of Australia in 20,000 BC were descendants of the first man, the 'man' of Genesis 1:26 but they were not the descendants of 'the man' of about 13,000 BC who was Cain's father.

From about Genesis 4:17 onwards we have reached the time when we can compare what we read with the history of the human race known from 'ordinary' historical study. In Genesis 1–3 it is difficult to correlate those events with other sources of history, but from Genesis 4 onwards our story can be studied alongside the earliest history of mankind that we know from other sources.

The genealogies of Genesis 5 and 10 may well have gaps in them, but it is not possible to push the date of Genesis 4 back to 100,000 BC or even 30,000 BC. The first period in the Bible which can be given a rough date with tolerable certainty is the time of Abraham (about 2000 BC). Terah (Genesis 11:27–32) must be dated at about 2135–1925 BC. Working backwards, the period covered by Genesis 10:1–11:26 must stretch from about 5000–2135 BC (as I shall argue). The time of the flood (Genesis 6:9–9:28) seems to be about 5600–5000 BC. Genesis 4:1–5:32 must cover a lengthy period, possibly from 13,000–5600 BC roughly. The date of Genesis 4:1 must be somewhere around 13,000 BC. Genesis 1–3 covers all the history of the universe before that time.

The Bible has its setting in real events, but by the time we have got to Genesis 4:1 the story has narrowed down. First it was the heavens and earth (1:1), then it was just the earth (1:2–2:3). Then it was the human race in the garden of Eden (2:4–3:24). At 4:1 it narrows even more. We are now in the Mesopotamian world, and we are looking at two brothers that come from 'the man' and from 'She who gives life'.

# Footnotes

[1] Genesis 1:27; 2:7 (twice); 2:8, 15, 16, 18, 19 (twice), 20, 21, 22 (twice), 23, 25; 3:8, 9, 12, 20, 22, 24; 4:1.

[2] Perhaps the vowel-pointing should be not *le'adam* but *la'adam*. The difference between 'Adam' and 'the man' depends at this point not on the consonantal text but upon the vowel-pointing – which was not part of the original text but was added much later.

# Chapter 23

## Cain and Abel

(Genesis 4:1–7)

Adam's sin leads on to murder between brother and brother (Genesis 4:1–16), and then to the decay of society (4:17–26). The world continues under a reign of death (5:1–32) and then becomes vulnerable to demonic powers (6:1–8). Sin operates in many directions. At first it results in a wrong relationship to God. Eve and then Adam refused the rule of God in their lives. Then sin damages us within. After Adam sinned he showed fear and guilt. Then the power of sin extends outwardly. In the story of Cain and Abel, there is hatred and animosity and jealousy reaching out to others. Once Adam and Eve had sinned against God, their children began to sin against each other.

1. **The human race divides into two**. One can see the 'seed of the woman', a section of the human race who would conquer the serpent. The 'seed' is both One and it is many. It is the Saviour and it is all of His people. There is also the 'seed of the serpent', a section of the human race who would be allied to the serpent and his hatred of God. Eve has two children (4:1–2a). One is acceptable to God; the other is not (Genesis 4:4–5).

2. **Everyone is aware of God**. Both sons in the family of Adam and Eve felt the need to worship God. The saved

and the lost, those who believe in a Saviour and those who do not, both parts of the human race, want to worship God. Cain brings an offering, Abel does the same (4:2b–4a). Even ungodly people want God's help.

3. **Everyone falls into one of two ways of worshipping God**. Here are two brothers. Their circumstances are similar. They are children of the same parents. Yet one is acceptable to God; the other is not (Genesis 4:4, 5). What makes the difference?

Consider **Abel**. He brings something from the flock, and God accepts him and approves of his offering. Abel wants to worship God, so he feels he should bring an animal, sacrifice it, and approach God in that way. He has faith in his heart that this is what God wants (see Hebrews 11:4).

He feels that he needs a substitute. He takes an animal and kills it, and he comes to God in this way. The idea came from what God had done according to Genesis 3:21. God had killed an animal and covered the nakedness of Adam and Eve. By the death of an animal came a covering of their shame. Abel follows this hint from God. He wants his shame to be covered also. He is aware of his sinfulness. He feels that an animal would be a good substitute. The animals were made on the same day as man, on the 'sixth day'. Man and the animals have a lot in common. Abel believes that an animal will act as a substitute for men – just as God suggested.

He feels that sin deserves to be punished. The death of this animal will serve as a sign that sin should be punished. Abel was admitting his need. He has faith in an atonement. The wages of sin is death (Genesis 3:19), but he believes the animal's death will be accepted for him. So the animal dies for the sins of Abel, and God allows Abel to approach him in this way. Abel is believing that God will accept him if he has faith in the death of a substitute.

God accepted animal-sacrifice before Jesus came. The

animal-sacrifice is a picture of what God will do through Jesus. Abel was the one who started by faith the sacrificial system, and he expressed his faith in this way. It pointed to the future. Jesus is our substitute. He lived the life we should have lived. He died as if He were a sinner. He had done nothing wrong, but He was dying in our place. The way of salvation is to have faith in a substitute, to trust in One who has lived for us and died for us. As soon as we trust that substitute we are acceptable to God.

Now consider **Cain**. If an animal spoke of substitutionary punishment, what did the fruit of the ground speak of? It spoke of hard work! God had said that the fruit of the ground could only come *'in the sweat of your face'* (Genesis 3:19). Cain wanted to worship God, but he brought the fruit of the ground. There was no question of the death of a substitute in that. Vegetable-offering is not a good substitute for man, and cannot forfeit its life. On the other hand growing food from the ground was associated with a lot of toil (Genesis 3:18–19). God had emphasized that very point. Cain's offering was an expression of salvation by works! It was his way of expressing his feeling that if he consecrated his labours to God, God would accept him in that way. But this is the way of the 'seed of the serpent'. This is the religion of the 'natural man' who wants to justify himself before God by his own good works. But salvation is not by good works (Ephesians 2:8–10; Romans 3:20, 22–24, 28; 4:4–6). Cain is saying to God 'I have done all this for you. Won't you receive me because of this hard work that I am presenting to you?'

There are two types of religion. All man-made religion begins by 'justification by good works'. Cain's approach to God is not a matter of faith. He brings an offering symbolizing his efforts and his good deeds. He presents an entirely different kind of offering. But it is the wrong way to come. 'Good works' is not the way of approaching God.

In Abel faith was expressed in animal-sacrifice. Abel was enabled to see that salvation would be by substitution. If we trust Jesus we shall be accepted too. God will acknowledge us and He will accept our offering – the blood of His Son.

# Chapter 24

## Two Ways to God

### (Genesis 4:1–16)

Cain and Abel are still with us. There are still two ways of approaching God. There are still the spiritual children of Cain. 'I am a churchman, I come to such-and-such church, I repent of my sins, I am doing my best, I am really quite a decent person'. It is the religion of Cain still!

1. **Cain was very self-confident**. He became angry that God had not received his worship (Genesis 4:5b). We like to save ourselves in our own way. We like to be right with God by our good deeds, and present our labours to God. Though Cain was a sinner he thought he could be acceptable to God by his good works, and rejected any idea that he needed an atonement.

2. **He chose his own way of approaching God**. Abel was following the hint that God had given in Genesis 3:21. Cain's way was purely self-invented.

3. **Cain's religion used ritual as a means of evading God**, but his heart was not right with God. His sacrifice was a routine to make him feel safe but he had no real interest in the Lord and His ways with mankind.

4. **Cain was characterized by hostility against God** (4:6). He resented his treatment by God. This is the way it is with all of the seed of the serpent. They are at enmity with God (Romans 5:10; 8:7; 2 Corinthians 5:20), and need

reconciliation with God. Yet God offers a way of salvation to Cain. 'If you do well, is there not a lifting up?', says God (4:7). It is an offer of forgiveness. A 'lifting up' means forgiveness. 'If you do well there is forgiveness, relief'. But Cain was not interested.

5. **Because Cain rejected God's way of salvation he became enslaved to sin**. God warned him. *'Sin is crouching at the door'* (4:7). It is like a wild animal ready to pounce and devour us. Cain finds sin to be more powerful than he imagined.

6. **This all comes out in bitter hatred of God's people**. Cain pretended to be friendly with Abel, invited him to a lonely spot,[1] and killed him. Abel had not done anything against Cain, but Cain's guilty conscience causes persecution. The 'seed of the serpent' will always be against those accepted by God. The greater the guilt, the greater the persecution. True faith rouses the hostility of the world. Cain did not like it that Abel was accepted by God but he himself was not. It led him to jealousy and murderous feelings within his heart towards Abel.

Cain has a kind of religion! He feels it would be useful to have God's blessing in his life. He wants to have dealings with God. Yet he is not acceptable to God because he will not come humbly, and in faith. Abel's faith is the only way. Man-made religion always leads to hatred and animosity towards Christians. Faith leads to righteous deeds (1 John 3:12, *'his brother's deeds were righteous'*) but righteousness only rouses resentment in the heart of Cain. There will always be this hatred and jealousy in the 'seed of the serpent', even though it can be covered over with a lot of superficial respectability and niceness.

What is the attitude of God towards Cain? It is frank and straightforward, and yet it is full of love.

God tells Cain his sin cannot be hidden (Genesis 4:9).

Cain tries to hide it. *'I do not know'*, he says, *'Am I my brother's keeper?'* But the blood cries from the ground (4:10). God knows all about it. Murder is a very serious sin. Blood cries out. Sin cannot be covered up from God. It can be hidden from people, but not from God. Cain has probably buried Abel in some lonely spot, but the blood still cries from the ground. Our sins cannot be hidden from God. They go on crying out until they have been dealt with. They can only be dealt with by faith and confession.

Before the fall Adam had toiled the ground easily. Then it became harder (3:18). Now Cain is excluded from working from the ground at all, and is banished to a different part of God's world. He becomes a wanderer. God is a holy God, and sin brings God's displeasure. Sin will find us out. It may be covered for a long while but eventually it comes out (4:11–12).

Despite what Cain has done there is mercy for him. He is in an agony about his punishment and fears that he too will be killed (4:13–14). He does not fear sin but he fears the consequences of sin. The killer fears being killed.

But God says He will protect Cain and keep him alive, giving him further opportunity to come to faith. God ordains some kind of sign to prevent Cain from being killed. We do not know what the 'sign' was. Some think it was a mark of some kind on Cain himself. Others – and I agree with them[2] – think it is some sign in the external world, such as an intensified fear of killing another human being.

God is not willing that any should perish, and leaves the way open for Cain to come back to Him. Perhaps Cain might believe after all.

Despite the opportunity given him, Cain *'went away from the presence of the LORD'* (4:16). He had salvation offered to him, but he went away. He begins to live a pagan life. He marries. He builds a city. He lives without reference to God. There is no evidence that God ever spoke to him again.

God still waits, still gives us a chance. He asks us to admit our need. The way of salvation is the same; it is to believe in a substitute. We can never progress beyond that. It is the only way to know God.

## Footnotes

[1] The Samaritan Pentateuch reads *'Let us go into the field'*. This is supported by ancient versions and is apparently original.

[2] The word 'sign' elsewhere mainly refers to an external event (Exodus 10:2, and elsewhere).

# Chapter 25

## 'Civilisation'

(Genesis 4:17–19)

The next phase of the story brings us to the rise of what we call 'civilisation'. 'Civilisation' was first established in six centres of the world (see Map 3).

**i.** The world's oldest known civilisation developed in '**Mesopotamia**'. The descendants of Cain and Seth, and the descendants of Noah, lived in this area. To them it was 'the earth'. Genesis 4 finds its setting in the 'New stone

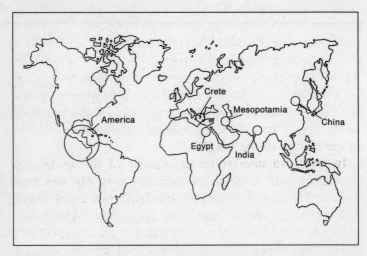

*Map 3:    The first six civilisations*

110

age' culture which arose in Mesopotamia. Civilisation in that area is recognizable to historians from about 5000 BC and Genesis 4:17–24 lets us know its beginnings were even earlier. The 'Sumerian' culture, which was well established by 3500 BC, is the first civilisation that historians are able to study in some detail with the aid of written records.

There were other civilisations that started soon after.

**ii.** In **Egypt** there were people hunting, fishing and gathering crops in 5000 BC, and Egypt became a kingdom under its first king in about 3200 BC.

**iii.** Neolithic culture reached **India** in about 4000 BC and the first Indian civilisation began in about 2500 BC.

**iv.** Towns were being built in **Crete** in about 2500 BC and civilisation there was well established by 2000 BC.

**v.** In **China** there is evidence of agriculture from about 5000 BC and the first Chinese civilisation dates from about 1700 BC.

**vi.** Further away there was a civilisation that began in **the American continent** (from about 1500 BC onwards). After about 1500 BC there were no new civilisations that emerged independently of the rest of the world.

Genesis chapters 1–11 concentrates on only one of these civilisations. Everything in these chapters is set in the world between the Tigris and the Euphrates, that is, in Mesopotamia. If we try to relate Genesis to what is known by historians we must say that Genesis 4:17ff tells the story of the rise of 'new stone age' culture in the first civilisation in the history of the world.

In trying to understand the history of the world and how it fits with Genesis, the difficulty is to discover how Genesis 3 links with Genesis 4. It is fairly sure that Genesis 4 describes the rise of 'new stone age' culture. The events of Genesis 4:17 onwards must be dated at about 13,000 BC. By the time we have got to Genesis 5:30 we have reached about 5600 BC. 'Civilisation' brought many blessings, yet it is also the story of the human race continuing to fall into deeper disobedience and hatred. Even though Cain has been wicked and murderous he continues to live, and from him and his children come the early civilisations of the Mesopotamian valley.

1. **Marriage and childbirth continues** (4:17). Cain has a wife and one of his children is named Enoch. God allows the human race to continue despite its sinfulness.

2. **We have the rise of cities** (4:17). The earliest city known to historians is Jericho. But Cain built a city even earlier, and named it after his son, Enoch. It is interesting that cities arise in the line of the wicked Cain. Cities arise when people want to congregate together, often for self-centred reasons. People are dissatisfied and fearful. They want to be near other people so that they can feel safe. Yet when they build cities and congregate together the city turns out to be not so wonderful after all! Despite the fact that people can crowd together, cities can be dangerous and lonely places. They can be places of violence and poverty. The city seems to offer security but then it turns out to be a place of threats and hazards. Cain's building a city was an attempt to overthrow the curse of Genesis 4:14. He had been condemned to a life of vagrancy and loneliness, and he was attempting to overthrow God's judgement on him. Yet he did not succeed. Cities do not provide the protection and safety that they are intended to provide.

3. **We have the first mention of polygamy in the Bible**. In the line of Cain, after Enoch comes Irad, then Mehujael, then Methushael, and then Lamech (4:18), and Lamech becomes the first polygamist to be mentioned in the Bible.

Again, it is interesting that polygamy arises in the line of Cain. It was a lapse from God's original plan. Again it is an attempt by the human race to defy God's way of doing things. Polygamy is not the same as promiscuity. It is a form of marriage. Yet it is a step down from God's ideal. It leads either to jealousies or to a lack of close family life. It began in the line of Cain.

The human race tries to find peace and satisfaction in the natural blessings of life. Childbirth, city-life, marriage and sexuality – these are blessings that God has given to the human race. They are part of His general goodness to all men. God is good to everyone and causes His sun to shine on the just and the unjust.

Yet these 'common blessings' of the human race have two limitations to them. They get misused by sinners. The descendants of Adam were furnished with these earthly and ordinary blessing, yet as we shall see, they used them only in the interests of sin.

It follows that a further limitation to the 'common blessings' is that they can never bring salvation. Men and women try to find peace and satisfaction and security in marriage, in building communities, in pressing for more and more sexual pleasures. But there is no salvation in these things and they let us down if we look to them to provide more than they are able to provide. The people of Cain continue to deteriorate despite God's goodness to them.

The thing that is missing is mentioned in Genesis 4:26. *'People began to call upon the name of Yahweh'.* It is calling upon God that brings salvation. Otherwise we have the blessings but not the Giver of them. And when you have the blessings but not the Giver of them, the blessings turn out to be not so marvellous after all. Families! Cities! Wives! But there will be no blessing in such things unless there is a calling on the name of Yahweh as well.

## Chapter 26

# Common Grace, Special Grace

### (Genesis 4:20–26)

God did not exterminate the world. He gave plenty of time and plenty of room for them to develop and do what they could to improve their lives. He showed mercy on them and allowed them to try to get honour for themselves, as they sought to make themselves a name (see 4:17).

4. **Next comes the development of various technologies**. Animal husbandry begins (4:20). Even among ungodly people God allows development and progress. It is part of His kindness to the entire human race. However there is no salvation in these blessings. The ungodly still are loved by God, and they develop skills and may show great cleverness in technology and in business. Yet for all their cleverness they never discover salvation. Salvation has to be over-and-above God's general kindness in allowing the human race to develop. There has to be something over-and-above nature.

5. **Artistic developments commence**. We have here the beginning of the making of musical instruments. Jubal played two musical instruments and many followed him (4:21). At the same time metal-work began in the story of the human race (4:22).

This is all part of what is sometimes called God's 'common grace'. God keeps life going. He shows kindliness to all men whether they are saved or not, allowing various beneficial developments to take place. It keeps the world going. God does not want it to perish prematurely. Society continues.

Yet Genesis 4 is also the story of increasing degradation. Look at the way in which music and culture are used (4:23–24). Lamech writes a piece of poetry, but what an ugly piece of poetry it is! It is a song. One can easily see the way its lines are parallel and poetical.

> *'Adah and Zilliah, listen to my voice*
> *You wives of Lamech, give heed to my speech'*

Lamech is singing this song. But what is he singing about? It is about polygamy (*'you wives of Lamech'*), about murder (*'I have slain a man'*), about revenge (*'If Cain is avenged ... Lamech is avenged seventy-seven times'*). This is how men and women use their 'culture'. God allows family-life and music and technology, but how does man use God's blessings? There is great kindness on God's side, yet men and women misuse everything God gives to them.

Lamech seems to want to be a greater murderer than his ancestor Cain (4:24). It is a song about murder and violence, a 'sword-song'. God allows the makers of musical instruments to arise, but they misuse their very culture to promote violence.

Music is wonderful. Think of the music of David and his beautiful psalms, and the poetry of the prophets. Yet music can be used for wicked purposes also. The ungodly are more inventive than the godly. Their inventiveness often comes because they are dissatisfied and in their restlessness they seek for something new. The human is falling into deeper savagery, and increased degradation. Lamech kills someone and delights in it. There are now no regrets about the punishment of sin (contrast 4:13). The human race left to itself declines.

Genesis 4:25–5:32 now introduces us to the line of Seth. There was special grace as well as common grace. The man Adam had another son (4:25) and there was another section of the human race that was not as ungodly as the line of Cain. Not every descendant of Seth was saved, but most of the believers were in this line. Seth had a descendant called Enosh (4:26) and it was at the time of Enosh that public worship of Yahweh began. God was keeping his 'church' alive. There were from time to time people who trusted in Him and in His promise that salvation would come and that 'the snake' would be crushed.

The line of Cain began to come together in cities, and it led to murder, polygamy, violence. But people in the line of Enosh also came together, not for murder, but for worship. There will always be the 'seed of the woman'. Seth was a replacement for Abel. God's line of believers cannot be exterminated. Abel may be killed but Seth replaces him. God will raise up others.

The great mark of the people of God is prayer. Here is the first description of corporate prayer in the Bible. Three aspects of prayer are notable.

(i) It is to be fervent. People call out, cry out. It is not some quiet respectable 'saying a prayer' but an energetic calling out to God.

(ii) It is corporate. People help each other when they come together to pray. Private prayer is alright, of course, but we can get into wandering ways and neglectful ways. Praying with others helps private praying just as private praying helps praying with others.

(iii) Prayer lays hold of God's character. They were calling on *'the name of Yahweh'*, appealing to the way He has revealed Himself. **In** prayer we lay hold of God's goodness, His mercy, His compassion. This is what it means to call on His 'name'. They called on the name of

116

'Yahweh' (sometimes spelt as 'Jehovah' or 'the LORD'). It is God's special name. It means *'HE IS'*, and is the name which would be especially explained later, in the days of Moses. It is associated with God as Saviour and Redeemer. Men and women at this time began to call upon the name of their Saviour-God. And it was not only groups who prayed like this. The story also tells us of individuals who walked with God and who found grace in God's eyes (5:24; 5:32; 6:8). Man has sinned terribly and disastrously but the kingdom of God goes on. God is still on the throne and He has His people who trust Him and live for Him.

# *Chapter 27*

# Life in the Midst of Death

(Genesis 5:1–32)

The genealogy from 'Man' to Noah is now presented. First, **let us consider the genealogy itself**. It shows that the story of the human race goes on. There is a connection between Noah and the people of Genesis 1–4.

(i) The genealogies are probably not complete. In Genesis 5 and Genesis 10 the same rounded number of segments suggests it was deliberately composed, picking out ten of the significant sections of the family line.

(ii) It is likely that the interpretation of the very long ages is partly to be explained by the assumption that names **sometimes** stand for segments of the family line. *'When Man* (or 'Adam') *had lived for 130 years he had a son...'* (5:3) may well be a Mesopotamian way of saying: 'At one point in the distant past the oldest family-line known went on for 130 years and then there came some-one who had a son who started a new section of the family line...'. There is evidence that ancient genealogies could work like this. It is quite certain that 'A begat B' can mean 'A begat a line ending in B'. The long lifetimes also are an ancient way of speaking. In Mesopotamian king-lists we have kings with fantastic ages, but the kings are known to have actually existed. In the 'unimportant' patches it is likely that a name stands for a segment of the genealogical line.

(iii) The gaps in the genealogy cannot be too big. A date of 1,000,000 BC for Cain (for example) would be impossible.

(iv) The ten names pick out key men, tell the age at which they begat the most significant of their sons, and the length of the line before another key-figure is considered.

(v) The ten segments of genealogy in Genesis 5:1–32 cover about 8000 years (the approximate sum). If these are the accounts of 'lines' rather than individuals, then the dates of the whole genealogy runs from about 13000 BC to about 5600 BC (the latter date depending on the interpretation of Genesis 10 yet to be given). If there are some gaps it could go back somewhat earlier. How far back is uncertain, but not tens of thousands of years.

Secondly, let us consider **the implications of the genealogy**.

It shows **God's faithfulness**. God had commanded the human race to multiply (1:28). Despite the sin of man God has not withdrawn the possibility of continuing to multiply upon the earth. Between Genesis 5:1 and 5:32 there are 8,000 years at least, maybe more, in which God had allowed humankind to continue.

It shows **the greatness of the fall of humankind**. The chapter begins by reminding us of what was at the beginning of man's story. He was made in the likeness of God (5:1–2). But then the rest of the chapter tells us to what depth he has descended. Genesis 2:16 has been fulfilled: 'And he died ... and he died ... and he died' is the dominant note of the chapter.

It shows **human inability to defeat death**. The running phrase of the chapter, 'And he died ... and he died', shows that despite the great technology and achievements of humankind recorded for us in Genesis 4:17–24 and despite the spirituality of Genesis 4:25–26, man still cannot rise above the curse of death.

It shows **that fellowship with God is the way of triumphing over the curse of the fall**. There are ten segments of genealogy: Adam – Seth – Enosh – Kenan – Mahalalel – Jared – Enoch – Methusalah – Lamech – Noah. The phrase 'And he died' comes eight times and Genesis 9:28 makes a ninth. Once the phrase is conspicuously absent. Enoch did not die (Genesis 5:21–24)! Enoch's triumph began in fellowship with God. He *'walked with God'*, that is, he went through life, step-by-step in fellowship with God.

Amidst that fellowship he was given a promise. Enoch did what he did 'by faith' and faith is always related to promise. By faith and patience we inherit promises (Hebrews 6:12). Somewhere in the days of his fellowship with God, God revealed to him that He did not wish Enoch to die. Amidst the endless dying that had gone on for thousands of years God planned to give a demonstration of His power over death. And Enoch believed God! *'By faith Enoch was taken up . . .'* (Hebrews 11:5).

In Enoch, God gave a glimpse of what redemption is and what it would mean for the snake to be crushed. The hope for the human race would be exemption from the curse of death altogether. The day will come when *'there will be no longer any death'* and the first things of our fallen world will have passed away – Satan included (Revelation 20:14; 21:5). The hope of total deliverance from the curse of the fall includes a restored fellowship with God and the total abolition of death. Enoch had the privilege of giving the world a glimpse of it. He went into God's presence without his body dying. He had the same experience that all Christians shall have who are alive at the time when Jesus comes – glorification without having a funeral first!

Enoch's story is a hint to us that what is needed in life is not great knowledge but simple faith. Enoch had little knowledge of what would come in the centuries ahead of him. Paul's epistles were not available to him. The life of Jesus was unknown to him. He did not even have the examples of David and Abraham. There were no great heroes of faith to be a model to him, except perhaps Abel. Yet his triumph over death was one of the greatest achievements ever. Only Elijah would ever repeat it. It is a demonstration to us that if we have a word from God, and if we believe, nothing is impossible for us.

# Chapter 28

# Sons of God and Daughters of Men

(Genesis 6:1–8)

The deterioration of humankind into sin now comes to its greatest climax in the Bible. Genesis relates the outworking of sin. Men and women were not originally sinful, but we have seen how they sinned against God (Genesis 3), against each other (Genesis 4), and of how sin damaged society.

Now we have a further stage in deterioration, the greatest yet and the greatest ever. *'It happened that when men began to multiply on the face of the land, and daughters were born to them,* (verse 2) *that the sons of God saw that the daughters of men were beautiful; and they took wives for themselves, whomever they chose'.* There was a population explosion in this part of the world. And at that time this calamity took place.

There are three ways in which this passage has been taken.

**i.** Some have thought the 'sons of God' means the line of Seth. But this is not the natural meaning of 'sons of God'. And why is it only godly men who marry ungodly women? Did not godly women and ungodly men marry? And should we believe that only Cainite daughters were good-looking?

**ii.** Another view is that the 'sons of God' are some kind of upper class, perhaps kings, who took large numbers of wives.

**iii.** A third view is that this refers to something very mysterious which took place in the world of angels. 'Sons of God' refers to angels. This is the view I think is right. The phrase 'sons of God' in Hebrew refers to angels (see Job 1:6; 2:1; 38:7 which refers to a time when there were no human beings; Psalm 29:1; 89:6).

This event is mentioned in 1 Peter 3:19–20, 2 Peter 2:4 and Jude 6 where it is interpreted as referring to angels.

It might be asked: can this happen? Can angels marry people? Remember these points.

**i.** Angels may look like men (Genesis 18:2, 8; 19:1, 5). They may be dressed like men; they may eat and drink. The men of Sodom tried to physically molest angels.

**ii.** We are dealing with the pre-flood world. Great changes came in the world after the flood, including changes in the angelic world. After the flood a restraint was put upon fallen angels. Matthew 22:30 is true **now**. It may not have been true **then**. The main point here is that sin in gigantic proportions came into the Mesopotamian world, leading to the end of the world for Mesopotamia. Perhaps (for all we know) similar things happened elsewhere. An event even greater than that of Genesis 3 took place, and once again *'they saw'* ... something *'good'* ... *and took'* – as in Genesis 3:6. Men and women continued to fall ever more deeply into sin. There came a point where they were vulnerable to attack by evil spirits. The world of evil angels got a grip on human life. Immoral relationships of a weird kind came into being. Angels saw human women and (perhaps via demon possessed men) marriages took place between them.

*'Then Yahweh said, "My spirit shall not abide in man forever, because he indeed is flesh. His days shall be one hundred and twenty years'* (6:3).

It made God determine that the 'spirit of life' should not dwell in men and women for such a lengthy period. (The AV 'strive' is not accurate.) The 120 years period either means that the life-span is to be reduced or (as I believe) that there are 120 years before the flood. Reference to the Lord's patience in 1 Peter 3:20 seems to confirm the second interpretation.

'*The Nephilim were also on the earth in those days, and also afterwards...*' (6:4). The word 'Nephilim' means 'fallen ones' and seems to refer to people who are fallen in society, 'criminals'. They were there even before the angel-marriages but the angel-marriages made things worse. The main point is that men and women tend to deteriorate morally and spiritually.

Genesis tells of God's attitude to the deterioration.

**He notices it** (6:5). Yahweh saw the wickedness of people was great. God is not far away so that He takes no notice of what is happening.

**God grieves** (6:6). Can God suffer? Does God have feelings? God suffered when men and women sinned.

**God judges sin** (6:7). He resolves to wipe out of existence both man and His world.

**God provides a way of salvation**. Noah found grace. God chose a man who would provide a way of salvation. 'Found grace' means that Noah did not deserve to be used by God. It was God's grace that saved him. Noah was to be a saviour, a means of salvation. When the judgement came there was to be a means of deliverance.

Man still deteriorates. Society still runs down unless God intervenes. God still sees, still takes note, still grieves over the world, still feels for man in his crisis and tragedy. He still judges sin and still resolves that the world will not go on for ever.

There will be an end to our world as there was to Noah's world. A saviour was chosen then; a Saviour is available now: Jesus Christ! Jesus has provided a way of salvation, as Noah provided an ark. Men and women are invited to go in. *'As it was in the days of Noah so shall it be ...'*

Jesus died on the cross, and paid a price for our sins. They had to trust in Noah's ark. We have to trust in Jesus' cross. They had to get inside the ark. We have to 'get inside' Jesus' cross. Jesus will be to us what Noah was to those in the ancient world. When we go in to Jesus He will keep us safe.

# Chapter 29

# The Flood
## (Genesis 6:9–7:5)

Uninhibited sin gets progressively worse until it brings down God's judgement. Genesis 6–9 tells us something of what that judgement is like, and lets us know that in the midst of judgement God is merciful and sends a way of salvation.

1. Consider, first, **God's saviour, Noah**. Noah was a righteous man, by means of his faith. *'By faith Noah being warned by God ... prepared an ark ... He became an heir of the righteousness which is by faith'* (Hebrews 11:7). God's Word came to him. God told Noah about the coming judgement and how Noah himself should make a way of rescue for all who would have faith. Noah believed God. That is what faith is; it is believing God. So Noah was right with God by faith.

He was *'blameless in his generation'* (6:9). He lived in terrible days. The world around him was degraded and depraved, yet Noah was blameless in the midst of it all. Despite the corrupt society all around him he remained clean and upright.

He had fellowship with God. He *'walked with God'*, says the Bible (6:9). This means that he had daily step-by-step fellowship with God. He had God as his companion as he walked through life.

Noah was also a family man. He had three sons (6:10). So Noah's godliness was the godliness of a man who was involved in ordinary life. He did not withdraw from society. Real godliness is not like that. Noah was out and about in God's world. He had the responsibilities of looking after a family.

This was the man that God used. It all started with the sheer grace of God. Noah is like Jesus. Jesus made a way of salvation by His perfect righteousness. Noah's godliness was not perfect, but Jesus lived a life of total sinlessness. God uses godly people, and the greatest of His servants was Jesus, His own Son. He had to be entirely sinless, in order to be our Saviour. Noah was the temporary saviour who kept his civilisation going until the final saviour should come.

2. Consider, next, **God's judgement**. God decided to give the human race another 120 years, giving humankind one last opportunity. God is slow to judge. His judgement comes at the end of a time-limit. The earth had become corrupt and violent (6:11). It affected the entire human race (although our story probably focuses on the Meso-potamian civilisation). The race had corrupted its way (6:12); the world had come to an end-point. Sin could get no worse. God resolved to annihilate almost all of that world (6:13).

God tolerated the sin of the human race for a long time. While the ark was being built Noah was telling the people of what God thought about sin. He was a *'preacher of righteousness'* (2 Peter 2:5). So God decided to judge 'the earth' or 'the land' (the Hebrew can be translated either way). Noah was told to make an ark (6:14–17) because God would make a covenant promising to preserve Noah's descendants (6:18). Yet the entire world of that time, in the area where 'the world' was, was corrupted to the point where it could not be allowed to survive any longer.

When man sins, the world falls with him. When man is judged, his environment is judged also. So *'Every living thing of all flesh'* (6:19–20) would perish. No doubt the fish survived, and probably only the Mesopotamian world was involved, but God would bring universal judgement.

God still is a holy God. He still hates sin. He still is slow to judge. He watches the sin of man and warns that it will not be allowed to go on for ever. God tells the world what He will do. Our world will also come to an end. We have prior notice that the judgement of God is on its way.

3. Consider, thirdly, **God's amazing grace in the midst of judgement**. God told Noah to make a way of salvation, the ark. Noah is told to have food ready (6:21) so as to live in it with a sample of the animals of his world. All who came into the ark would be kept safe.

And this is what happened (6:22). It was a thorough provision. There were to be little rooms in it (6:14). It was to be a place which would give security when God's waters of destruction came.

This salvation was by faith. You had to enter it (7:1). That was all that had to happen for Noah and his family and a sample of his world to be kept safe (7:1–3). They were told what would happen (7:4) and what they should do. If they believed there was safety. Noah did what he was told and so he and all who went with him – seven other people – were brought safely through the judgement of God.

God has appointed a Saviour, the man Jesus Christ, who never sinned. Jesus was given instructions. On the cross He made a way of salvation. Salvation is still by taking a step of faith. At the end of the flood Noah's people would emerge into a new world. They had provision to keep them alive until they came through. We too take one step into Jesus, God's ark.

Noah had to tell others of what would happen (2 Peter 2:5). I suppose he was ridiculed, but he saved his family. *'By faith ... he built an ark for the salvation of his household'* (Hebrews 11:7). You may not be able to persuade many, but if you can persuade those near you to enter into God's ark, the Lord Jesus Christ, you have done something wonderful.

# Chapter 30

## Introducing 'Covenant'
### (Genesis 6:18)

God's act of saving Noah and his children through the ark in a time of judgement led into a 'covenant'. *'I will establish my covenant'*, said God (Genesis 6:18).

The idea of a covenant is an important theme in the Bible and we must consider it in more detail.

1. Consider first of all **faulty definitions of 'covenant'**. It is not enough to think covenant is simply an agreement. 'Covenant' is sometimes defined as though it were some kind of bargain but the subject must be understood more precisely than that. **A covenant is a promise which has an oath added to it**.

Take what happens in Nehemiah chapter 5, where the difference between promise and oath is made clear. Nehemiah complains that the Jews are ill-treating their poorer fellow-Jews. He is angry (Nehemiah 5:6) and calls a meeting in which he condemns them sharply for what they have done. The upper classes of Judea promise to restore the heavy interest they have taken when giving loans to their poorer brothers and sisters. Notice: they give a promise. *'We will restore everything and we shall demand nothing more from them'* (Nehemiah 5:12). But Nehemiah wants something more. He sends for the priests and makes the people take an oath. This is a covenant! A covenant is a promise that has been made secure by the taking of an oath. He leads them through a ceremony (Nehemiah 5:13) and gets them to swear that they will do as they have said. Once you have taken an oath you are legally committed.

2. We must realise that **there are three kinds of covenant**: covenants of obligation to a senior, covenants of generosity towards a junior, and two-way covenants between equals. In Genesis the word 'covenant' comes 27 times. On 22 occasions it is connected with divine generosity to the world through Noah (6:18; 9:9, 11, 12, 13, 15, 16, 17); or to Abraham's seed through Abraham (15:18; 17:2, 4, 7, 9, 10, 11, 13, 14, 19, 21). In five references (14:13; 21:27, 32; 26:28; 31:44) people who are equal make oaths to each other. Another kind of covenant, a covenant where a junior swears obedience to a senior, is not mentioned in Genesis; the first reference to such a covenant is in Exodus 19:5 (where people are to swear allegiance to God) and Exodus 23:32 (where the law forbade Canaanites to escape judgement by swearing allegiance to Israel).

Noah's covenant was a covenant of generosity. The covenant made with Israel via Moses on Mount Sinai was a law-covenant and we are not under it.

There are other covenants of generosity as well as that through Noah. Later in the Bible we have mention of covenants with Abraham, with David, and with Jesus and His people.

Thirdly, let us consider some of **the ingredients of covenants**.

**i.** A covenant has a promise.

**ii.** A covenant has an oath.

**iii.** A covenant may have a beneficiary, someone who is receiving the blessing of the oath. Or it may have an victim, a target, a person who is obliged to swear allegiance.

**iv.** A covenant of generosity is unconditional, after it has been given, although

**v.** it might be given as a reward.

**vi.** A covenant may take time to take place because it is not settled until the oath is given.

**vii.** A covenant may have attached to it a sign or symbol of some kind.

**viii.** A covenant involved the shedding of blood in some kind of sacrifice.

All of these ingredients are to be found in God's covenant with and through Noah.

**i.** The promise was that God said he would not destroy the world by water.

**ii.** Because it was a covenant God is in fact swearing an unbreakable oath. There are *'two unchangeable things'* (Hebrews 6:18), promise and oath.

**iii.** The 'beneficiary' was the entire world, Noah, his children, the animals, the very land itself.

**iv.** Once the covenant was given it could never be reversed. The sworn promises of Genesis 8:22 and 9:11 will never be cancelled.

**v.** The unconditional covenant was given as a reward. It was **after** Noah's obedience (6:22) that it was implemented.

**vi.** The covenant took some time. God made a proposal first (6:13–21) and then the covenant ceremony was after the flood (8:22).

**vii.** Attached to the covenant with Noah was the sign of the rainbow. The rainbow was a sign that God would keep his oath.

**viii.** The covenant with Noah was established upon the basis of sacrifice and the shedding of blood (8:20).

We can see many of these things in other covenants. God made a covenant with Abraham.

**i.** God gave promises to Abraham (Genesis 12:2–3).

**ii.** Later He started making a covenant (Genesis 15:1–21). God was preparing to take an oath.

**iii.** The one to receive the covenant-blessings was Abraham and his seed, his physical seed the Jews, his spiritual seed all believers.

**iv.** There came a point where the covenant could not be lost (it was after Genesis 22).

**v.** It was a reward for obedience.

**vi.** The covenant took time. The promises were given in Genesis 12 and 15; the oath was taken in Genesis 22.

**vii.** The covenant sign was circumcision.

**viii.** It involved sacrifice (Genesis 15:9–10).

The new covenant is parallel.

**i.** The covenant has a promise. The promise is the blessings of the Holy Spirit.

**ii.** We are in a relationship where God is offering to take an oath about these blessings. In Hebrews it is called *'entering into rest'*.

**iii.** The beneficiaries are believers and their seed on condition that they are saved (Acts 2:39).

**iv.** The blood of the covenant is the blood of Jesus Christ.

**v.** It takes time to enter rest.

**vi.** When God swears to us, the promise concerned will not be lost.

**vii.** The covenant-signs are baptism and the Lord's Supper.

**viii.** It takes effect by our depending on the blood of Jesus Christ.

These themes must be developed as we consider Genesis but we have them here in embryo. Genesis 6:18 announces a theme that will be taken up by the rest of the Bible.

# Chapter 31

## Saved for a New World
### (Genesis 7:6–8:19)

All the principles of judgement and of salvation through Jesus are to be found in these chapters.

1. **The flood is a fact of history**. It actually happened, probably round about 5000 BC. It is clear that records were being kept during the flood. Genesis 7:6 says Noah was 600 years old when it happened. That either means that at that stage people lived to an old age or it means that Noah's **family** was 600 years old. But the point is that someone was taking a note of the times and the dates. Genesis 7:10 tells us that the flood came seven days after they entered the ark. Again someone, probably Noah himself, must have been keeping a diary of events. The day when the flood waters began to burst out on to the earth is carefully recorded; it was on *'the six hundredth year ... the second month ... the seventeenth day'* (7:11). In Genesis 8:3–4 we are told how long it took for the waters to go down again, and how on the seventeenth day of the seventh month the ark rested at Ararat. The mentioning of the days continues in the following verses (8:5, 6, 10, 12, 13). This is history; dates were being kept. It actually happened. We do not know how extensive was 'the earth'. It may mean the Mesopotamian valley area. But it certainly was 'the world' so far as Noah was concerned. And certainly 'all flesh' in that world perished. When the

Bible talks about 'the world' it refers to the known extent of the civilisations around the Mediterranean world. Genesis 4–11 is relating events in Mesopotamia.

2. **The flood was a foretaste of God's judgement**. *'As it was in the days of Noah, so will be the coming of the Son of Man'* (Matthew 24:37). The old world was destroyed by *'a flood on a world of the ungodly'* (2 Peter 2:5; see 3:6). Similarly *'the present heavens and earth have been reserved for fire'*. God told Noah and his family to enter in (7:1–10). Then a number of days after, the flood waters came. All the springs of water beneath the land burst forth and the gates of heaven were opened (7:11–16). It rose higher and higher (7:17–24). Here in Genesis 7:11–24 we have God undoing what He did at creation. Sin leads to the undoing of creation. This is what God will do again. He will un-do our world. God will not allow sin to go on forever.

3. **In the middle of that judgement there was mercy**. God always shows mercy in the midst of wrath. He is not pure undiluted anger. He hates sin and judges it but that does not mean that God is wholly taken up with anger and judgement. In the middle of it there is mercy. Genesis 7:13 says *'On that very day'* – the day when waters burst forward – Noah and his sons and their wives entered the ark. They found a way of safety amidst the judgement of God all around them. It is still true that all who go in to Jesus, God's ark, find salvation, as they did in Noah's world. It is 'entered into'. We 'go in' to Jesus as they went in (7:13). They simply believed!

4. **Once Noah had entered he was safe**. The animals showed that God was starting again with a new world but that He was not starting a new creation altogether. This is God's way. He did not abandon the old world. He brought a bit of the old world through, recreated it, and started again. God's new creation is His refusal to abandon the old creation.

When Noah went in *'then the LORD shut him in'* (7:16). His security was God's responsibility. It was not Noah's task to keep himself in the ark. Once he was in, he was in! God keeps us safe. God closed the door. There was no possibility of Noah's falling out of that ark and not getting to the new world after all. God closes the door.

The flood kept coming (7:17). There was torrential downpour. There was no possibility of escape. The whole of Noah's world ended. The water went higher and soon rose above the hills. No one could get away. Judgement prevailed! So in our world, when judgement comes, the only place of safety will be in Jesus. These principles will be re-enacted all over again. All flesh died. There was universal death. The wages of sin is death. Sin brings penalty in one form or another, sooner or later. In 7:21–24 we are told how all the creatures that were in that part of the world were wiped out.

The judgement of God did not go on for ever. God remembered Noah (Genesis 8:1), and soon the waters were going down again (8:1–5) and the earth was getting dry (8:6–14). God was faithful to those who had put their trust in Him and His salvation and His saviour Noah. God is faithful to us. When we believe, Jesus keeps us riding above the storms of judgement. We shall come out alive the other side ready for God's new world.

5. **Salvation leads into newness of life**. Soon they receive the command to leave the ark (8:15–19). They come out into a world that has been cleansed and washed. It has no signs of the old wicked world before the flood. Noah and the animals are the start of a new stage of history. Life begins again for Noah and for those who have trusted God's salvation. These events give us a preview of what God will do again, not with water but with fire. We shall come out into a new heaven and into a new earth, into a new world where there is righteousness.

# *Chapter 32*

## The Rainbow in the Cloud
(Genesis 8:20–9:18)

A covenant is a promise that has been made unbreakable, at least in theory.

God binds Himself to keep His word. He made a covenant with Noah, with Abraham, with David, and (in a different kind of covenant), with Moses.

1. **The basis of covenant is sacrifice**. As soon as Noah was out of the ark, he built an altar to Yahweh (8:20) and, taking some of the clean animals he sacrificed burnt offerings. It was a way of expressing his dedication to God and his gratitude to God. Yet he could only approach God on the basis of a substitute dying for him.

God was pleased with the sacrifice (8:21a) and **after the sacrifice** gave a promise: never again would He curse the ground (see 8:22b). The seasons necessary for planting and harvesting would continue. Noah's salvation from drowning becomes the starting point of blessing for all humankind. The next time it rains they need not worry that the flood is being repeated.

Similarly, God offers promises to us in Jesus. He saves us and then promises that we shall inherit His blessings. We shall be enabled to serve Him. We shall experience God's protection and provision. We shall enter into a knowledge of God's will and participate in the forward development of God's kingdom. By faith in these promises and **on the basis of blood-atonement**, we go forward. Without the sacrifice of Jesus' blood there is no forgiveness, no starting-point. Without the sacrifice of Jesus' blood there is no daily cleansing, no receiving of provisions and enablings from above. The basis of covenant-relationship is blood-atonement.

2. **The covenant is full of promises for the future**. God commissions Noah to refill the land (9:1), and gives promises of safety (9:2) and provision (9:3). The only 'regulation' imposed on him concerns the shedding of blood. The blood of animals is to be treated as sacred (9:4) because of its use in symbolism when animals are sacrificed. And the crime of murder is to be treated as more serious than almost any other crime because of the sanctity of life (9:5). The number of people must increase (9:6). Noah must refill the land (9:7).

The new covenant promises are promises of what God will do for us in the course of our life. He promises the continuing presence of the Spirit. He will give us a new heart. He will lead us into godliness. He will open our minds and give us a knowledge of Himself and of His will.

As promises to Noah dealt with the future and the progress of God's world, so the promises to the Christian deal with the future and the progress of God's kingdom in us and through us. By faith and patience these promises have to be 'inherited'.

3. **God is sovereignly in control all the way through**. God takes the initiative. It was not Noah's idea to have this covenant. God said to Noah *'I am establishing my covenant with you...'* (9:8). It is a very emphatic statement. 'I am saying this', 'I will do this...', says God.

God maintains his leadership. He says 'I have saved you. Now I am giving you promises. I will do it for you. Your job is to trust me and to cooperate with me. Then I will bring you into a whole new realm that I am promising to give you ...'.

4. **This covenant embraced the whole world**. God would maintain His promise with all Noah's descendants (9:9). It would include the animals (9:10), and the entire human race, *'all flesh'* (9:11), it would last for all generations (9:12). Everyone born would be safe from any threat of a repeated flood.

God's covenants get narrower and more precise as they proceed in the history of the world. The first one was with every living creature and with planet earth. The covenant with Abraham was for Abraham and his descendants. The covenant with Moses would be narrower still, with the nation of Israel. The covenant with David would be only for David's line. The covenant with Jesus is even more precise; it is only for the saved. God is not in covenant with any unsaved person. Children are in the covenant only on condition that they have been called to salvation (*'you and your children ... as many as the Lord ... shall call'*, Acts 2:39). The covenants get progressively more precise. The covenant with Noah was for the entire cosmos. Even animals were involved.

5. **Once the oath was given it was unconditional**. There is no possibility that the promises of 8:22 will ever be reversed.

Similarly once God 'swears' to us, the blessings that have been sworn cannot be lost. The covenant through Noah was a reward for Noah's responsiveness, but once given it could not be lost. So it is about anything in which God takes an oath.

6. **The covenant had a mediator**. God chose to give these promises through Noah. He is speaking to Noah (in 8:21–22; 9:1b–7, 9–11,12–16,17) and he passes on what is said and others benefit through what God gives to him.

God says to Jesus *'I will give you the nations of the*

*world'*. Everyone who comes to Jesus is open to the promises of the covenant, but they cannot be found outside of Jesus.

7. **There was a covenant-sign, the rainbow**. There was something visible that recalled the promises (9:12–17). When you see a rainbow, says God, treat it as a sign that I am not judging the world. It is a sign that I am not judging the world with another flood. It is a sign of my mercy, a sign of my commitment to my oath.

God's 'covenant-signs' of baptism and the Lord's Supper are similar. They are signs of God's promises to us, promises that God will cleanse us and feed us for ever.

# Chapter 33

## Shem, Ham and Japheth

(Genesis 9:18–29)

The great hero of the flood, Noah, disgraces himself! He is a second Adam, and like Adam he is to populate the land, and be a farmer. Like Adam he falls because of his physical appetite, this time not for fruit from the tree but drink from the vineyard.

A small family came out of the ark (9:18), and God picked up again with the three sons and a grandson, Canaan. The Mesopotamian world and its surrounding areas is repopulated from these three lines (9:19). *'Noah, the man of the soil, began life again and planted a vineyard'* (9:20; to translate, 'Noah ... was the first farmer', is a mistake). He drinks some of its wine. Perhaps he was not aware of what would happen if he drank too much of it. In his grogginess he became uncovered in his tent (9:21). Ham takes pleasure in his father's degradation and spreads the tale of what had happened (9:22). He enjoyed what had happened, but the others do what they can to protect their father in a dignified manner (9:23).

Noah wakes up (9:24), finds out what had happened, thinks about Ham and the grandson Canaan, and is led by the Spirit to give a prophecy. It is the second Messianic prophecy of the Bible.

1. **We notice the honesty of Scripture**. It does not cover

up the sins of the saints. It is an embarrassing story, but the writer makes no attempt to disguise the fact that Noah was fallible. The Bible-writers are forgiving (no one's sin is mentioned in Hebrews 11) but they do not pretend the heroes of faith are faultless.

2. **The greatest of believers have weaknesses**. Even heroes of faith have sins. Not only Noah's drunkenness, but Abraham's deceit, David's adultery and murder, Peter's cursing, and the disastrous wanderings of Samson, and Jephthah, Solomon, and others, are all told to us. The Christian is not a super-saint. He is an ordinary person saved by grace. The people of God are upheld by God's grace. If we are different it is because of the powerful support of God. If we are not upheld we can fall at any moment. The only thing that makes us different is that we are sustained by God's mercy. If God should let us go we can slip badly. Who can say what we would do if God lets us go? And God can let us go for a while if we become proud.

3. **We are warned of the danger of wine**. The Bible does not absolutely forbid wine. There are no laws about it, but there are many warnings. *'Let every man be convinced in his own mind'* about the details of behaviour – but take warning!

Led by the Spirit Noah gives a prediction.

1. **Canaan is cursed**. Noah thinks about his child Ham who seemed to delight in sin. He thinks too about his grandson Canaan, and is led by the Spirit to see that this bad aspect of Ham's character is going to continue in Canaan. We remember the Canaanites! They became so vile and filthy.

This verse has been misused to justify discrimination against people who are reckoned to descend from Ham. But the writer is talking about Canaanites, not everyone from the line of Ham. In fact the Canaanites did become degraded and nations around dominated them. The Israelites conquered them later. It is certainly wicked to grade mankind into groups and then practise discrimination on that basis. Genesis 9:25 certainly cannot justify racism, and fortunately such racist interpretations are not heard much nowadays.

The gospel of Jesus overcame distinctions of this kind. There are no tribes, races, kindred, tongues, in Jesus. There is no Greek or Jew, circumcised, barbarian, Scythian. There is no slave or free person. Christ is in all.

2. **Shem is to be blessed**. He is told that out of his line will come great blessing (9:26). It is interesting that the name Yahweh is used. It means 'God who redeems by the blood of the lamb'. The prediction is Messianic. Noah is given a conviction that salvation and blessing will come through the line of Shem. In due course Jesus would be a Jew, a Semite, a descendant in the line of Shem through whom the entire human race will be blessed.

3. **Japheth is to have extended territory**. His line will not lead to the Messiah but there is blessing in store for him. He had protected Noah and will find protection himself. The language is picturesque. Japheth *'lives in the tents of Shem'*. One person is pictured as taking shelter with another. In the course of history salvation would come through a Semite – Jesus. Then an abundance of Gentiles would come to salvation through a Jewish Saviour. The people of Japheth were enlarged in their population and in their territory, but there is more involved here than territorial expansion. The gospel would come through a Semitic Saviour, and when He came salvation would be for all people everywhere. Many of the people of Japheth around the Mediterranean area would 'take shelter' in this Semitic Saviour.

The picture of salvation is slowly beginning to grow. The Saviour will be born of a woman (Genesis 3:15), a

Semite (9:26). We shall be told He will be of the tribe of Judah, a son of David, one born in Bethlehem, born of a virgin. The picture starts to grow here in Genesis 3 and 9, but will fill out more and more. Only Jesus fits the picture.

Meanwhile man's second chance did not stop his being a sinner. Noah was not unfallen Adam. And eventually Noah died. Genesis 9:29 completes the keynote of Genesis 5. Sin and death are still continuing, but the Saviour is on His way.

# Chapter 34

## The List of the Nations

### (Genesis 10:1–32)

After the flood, humankind gets another chance. God preserved the family of Noah and beginning with Noah's family, the story of the human race begins again. Noah's offspring spread all over the ancient Near East and even further.

Noah had three sons, Shem, Ham and Japheth (10:1). The human race in Mesopotamia expanded and tribes and nations came into being. Genesis 10 tells us the story of where they went to. The chapter gives a 'family tree', with gaps in it, to explain the presence of various nations in the ancient Near East, all of whom descended from Noah. The flood must have been local, since there were humans in other parts of the world. Genesis 10 deals only with the Mesopotamian world, but in 5000–2000 BC there were plenty of people in other parts of the world who get no mention in Genesis 10.

It deals with the period between Noah (maybe about 5000 BC) and Abraham (2000 BC), and beyond (for some of the nations are from the mid-second millenium, after Abraham). We have the lands which sprang from Japheth (10:2–5), and from Ham (10:6–20), and from Shem (10:21–31) (see Map 4).

Coming from Japheth various nations emerged in the

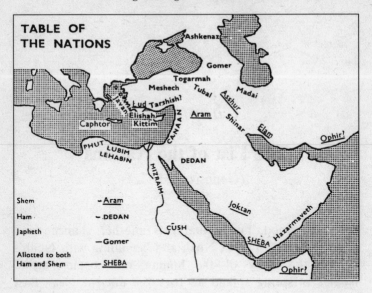

**TABLE OF THE NATIONS**

Ashkenaz

Gomer

Togarmah

Meshech · Tubal

Madai

Asshur

Lud · Tarshish?

Elishah · Aram · Shinar

Caphtor · Kittim

Elam

Ophir?

CANAAN

PHUT · LUBIM · LEHABIN

MIZRAIM

DEDAN

Joktan

Hazarmaveth

CUSH

SHEBA

Ophir?

| Shem | — Aram |
| Ham | — DEDAN |
| Japheth | — Gomer |
| Allotted to both Ham and Shem | SHEBA |

*Map 4: The table of the nations*

north. Coming from Ham nations emerged in the south-west including Egypt, Cush and the tribes of Canaan. Coming from Shem came nations in the direction of the south-east. Shem's line is traced to six generations, Ham's to four, and Japheth's to three. This section included the forebears of Israel. The word 'Semites' comes from Shem's name.

The 'table of the nations' must have been written some time in the 2nd millenium BC before it was incorporated into Genesis. 'Nimrod' perhaps dates in the middle of the second millenium.

1. **This piece of ancient Near Eastern history gives us a picture of rising imperialism**. Not much is said about Japheth's line (10:2–5), but out of Shem's line comes Cush (perhaps the same as Kish which is well-known to students of this period). From Cush came Nimrod, who is perhaps the same as Sargon of Accad who lived about 2300 BC.

146

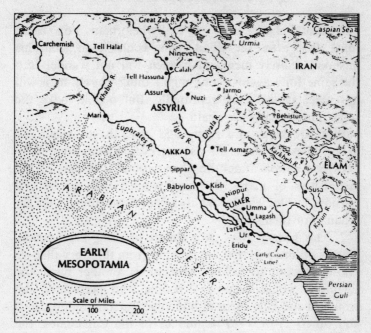

*Map 5:   Mesopotamia*

Nimrod – whoever he was – was the founder of a great empire which at first included Babylon, Erech, Akkad and Calneh, in the land of Shinar (i.e. Sumeria, Mesopotamia). Nimrod was an empire builder and warrior. He loved hunting. Babylonian and Assyrian kings are often pictured on the walls of ancient ruins as engaged in lion-hunting. Nimrod was perhaps the first of them, a warrior and hunter. He extended his empire to Assyria (10:11) and built Nineveh, Calah, and others (10:12) (see Map 5).

This is typical of powerful men. They like to ever extend their power and are greedy for more and more domains over which to rule. Nimrod was an imperialist, an empire-builder, ambitious to extend his kingdoms. The very name means 'We have rebelled' or 'Let us rebel'.

147

A second chance does not really help man. You would think that after the flood man would learn from his mistakes. 'Surely men and women will not wander into the same folly again' – one might think. Surely man will not rebel against God repeatedly. But people make the same mistakes all over again.

Why are kings and rulers and generals so ambitious? Where does this international aggression come from? Why does one nation attack another nation? It is part of the restlessness of man. Men and women wish to have a purpose in life. They want to achieve something, and get a name for themselves.

2. **This history gives us a picture of rising degradation**. Names occur to us that are familiar from the story that we know is about to follow. Mizraim is another name for Egypt; it would become a people who persecuted the Israelites and kept them in bondage. Canaan, Sidon, Heth and others (10:15–18) remind us of the Canaanites, the Sidonians, the Hittites and peoples who would one day come under God's judgement because of their degradation. Sodom and Gomorrah and nearby city-states (10:19) became famous for their perversity.

3. **This history points to the line of Shem as the one leading to the Saviour** (10:22–31). Japheth's line is traced to three generations, Ham's to four, but Shem's to six! This is because the story is moving rapidly towards Abraham in the line of Shem.

These were the nations that spread out in this part of the ancient world. It was in this near eastern world that the events of salvation would take place. The 'table of the nations' points in the direction of Abraham, and Abraham points us to the 'seed' of Abraham, Jesus our Saviour. There are seventy nations mentioned in Genesis 10. It is a kind of 'perfect number' in the thinking of ancient people. The seventy nations represented the entire world –

even though there were human beings outside of these seventy. Yet 'the world', represented by seventy nations, was only interested in aggression and expansion and self-interest.

On the day of Pentecost again the crowd represented *'every nation under heaven'* (Acts 2:5). A righteous empire could not be achieved by militarism but what militarism could not achieve would one day be achieved, not by a mighty hunter but by a mighty Saviour. It would lead not to the nations fragmenting into hostile kingdoms, but to representatives of the nations coming together to make a new empire, under the influence of the powerful Holy Spirit of God.

# Chapter 35

# The Tower of Babel

(Genesis 11:1–9)

After the flood separate tribes established distinct identities in the 'fertile crescent' (10:1). God was bringing nations into being but this also involved the bringing into being of distinct languages. The clans that became small nations in the 'whole earth' developed different languages and soon could not communicate with each other. Genesis 11:1–9 refers to a period that is covered by the genealogy of Genesis 11:10–32 which must amount to about 3000 years. The change was not necessarily a miracle of a few seconds.

We are watching **the rise of the 'state', which is another institution ordained by God**. Different nations are coming into being speaking different languages. We have seen how **marriage** was part of creation. And we may have noticed how God operates with families. The **family** of Noah was rescued with Noah, and the writer has drawn attention to the way in which both Enoch and Noah began families. These are structures of society through which God works. Now we have another one of these structures; nations are ordained by God too. Genesis 10 has referred to many small nations; now Genesis 11:1–9 goes into the linguistic side of the matter.

**God restrains sin by allowing division in the human race.** Genesis 11:1–4 pictures a further growth in human arrogance. We have seen it several times before. Men and women wanted to be like God (3:5) but brought disaster into humankind. Then there was a further attempt to break out of the realm in which God had put them. They became vulnerable to *'angels who did not keep their position'* (Jude 6). Again it led to terrible disaster and God brought the flood to wipe humankind off the face of the earth in that area. Now something similar is happening again. What will God do this time?

After the flood Shem's people had one language (11:1). Unity is a powerful source of effectiveness. Even without God a united people had great potential for achieving their hopes, but the hopes of these people were arrogant. They moved eastwards from the area of Ararat and reached the broad flat plains of the Mesopotamian valley between the rivers Euphrates and Tigris. 'Shinar' (11:2) is in the region of (or identical to) Sumeria or Mesopotamia.

Soon a powerful civilisation has arisen and again – for the third time in the book of Genesis – they want to ascend into heaven and get into God's paradise. A new kind of brick, and the strong adhesive that can be made from Sumerian soil, gives them a new idea (11:3). They started making a tower. Again the human race is inventive, but uses its inventiveness in the interests of ambition to become like God and satisfy a desire for fame. They want to maintain their unity but their aim is to overthrow the scattering that God has imposed on the nations (*'Fill the earth!'*, says 1:28 and 9:1). To the new civilisation 'Babel' meant 'Gate of God'. To a Hebrew speaker it sounded as if it meant 'Confusion'. The people wanted a gateway into the presence of God; our writer says 'All they got was confused languages and confused nations!'

The people of Shem have been given another chance but being given a 'second chance' by God brought no great change. They did not want to be scattered. They wanted to get into heaven in their own way, and were striving to get glory and a name for themselves, uniting in rebellion against God.

**God is continually watching over the sinfulness of human-kind** (11:5). He comes down to investigate. They were trying to get **high** to God, but so pathetic are their attempts God has to come **down** to even see it!

**God blocks all attempts to get to paradise that do not involve faith**. God was not willing for humankind to get to the dwelling-place of God in any way except through Jesus, the seed of Abraham. In order to curtail the sinful ambitions of the human race God introduces nations and gives them different languages. It will never be possible for the whole world to reach unity. Again and again, failures in communication block the way to worldwide unity. Languages restrain man from being as united as he wants to be. They prevent a successful worldwide anti-God movement. This linguistic and multinational distinctiveness hinders men and women from successfully rising against God. Maybe it always will.

At the first rebellion of humankind (Genesis 3), God excluded them from Eden. At the second rebellion (Genesis 6), God brought the flood. Now in a third rebellion, what will God do? The rest of the Bible will tell us the answer. He will start afresh with Abraham and through Abraham send Jesus in whom all nations will be blessed. Through Abraham God will provide the very thing that the human race wanted, a name for itself. *'I will make your name great'*, God will say to Abraham, and 'a name' in the book of life will be the Christian's reward.

The day of Pentecost is the reversal of the incident at Babel. Once again a representative selection of the world's nations were present (Acts 2:5; comparable to Genesis 11). Before 'languages' were given to divide, now 'tongues of fire' are given which gives 'languages' or 'tongues' and

Babel is reversed! Before a united people were divided by diversity of language; now they ask *'How is it each of us hears them in his own language'* (Acts 2:8)? If before it was a miracle of division, Pentecost was a miracle of unity – the very thing the early peoples wanted! But this world-wide unity comes through grace, not through nature, through God's coming down, not through man's climbing up. We never do climb up! When all is over and sin and wickedness and death and Hades are all thrown into the lake of fire, the new Jerusalem will come down (Revelation 21:2) and paradise will be restored.

# *Chapter 36*

# Approaching Abraham
### (Genesis 11:10–32)

This section of Genesis now moves rapidly to Abraham who will be the main character in Genesis and whose story will occupy a third of its space. We notice (1) that **thousands of years produced no great change in the human race**. In Genesis 11:10–26 we have a record of the family line leading from Shem to Abraham. It covers thousands of years, and people have been given a second chance to find a way of righteouness after the flood, but the second chance does not produce salvation. Humankind is not able to rise above its own sinfulness. Generation after generation comes and goes but no deliverance is found within humankind. At the end of the chapter we have a new name: Abraham (11:27)!

Abraham is God's answer to human wickedness. But we note (2) **Abraham came from a pagan family; God's new initiative was a matter of grace**.

Abraham's genealogy is like the one in Genesis 5, in that it has ten sections, with ten names, Shem, Arphaxad, Salah, Eber, Peleg, Reu, Serug, Nahor, Terah, Abraham. It is probable that names sometimes stand for segments of the family line. They are probably not overlapping except maybe at certain points of special interest. This means that a section of the line can be read as follows: **A** lived for

**x** number of years and had a son leading to the family of **B**. The family records show that there were **y** number of years before **B** was reached. This would mean that Genesis 11:14 really means 'There was a man in the family tree called Salah. When he was 30 years old he had a son and that son's line was to lead eventually to Eber'. Genesis 11:15 means: 'The line of Salah continued for a further 403 years. Then Eber was the next significant figure in this family-tree'.

If this is a correct way to read the genealogy, then it covers a period of nearly 3000 years. If we put Abraham's birth at about 2000 BC, the segments of genealogy would run from about 5000 BC to about 2000 BC.

This assumes that there are not **large** omissions in the genealogy. If there are largish gaps, the date of the flood could be pushed much further back. It could for example be as far back as the end of the ice-age at about 10,000 BC. Yet it is hard to imagine gaps in genealogy as big as this, so a later date is more likely than an earlier date. The flood was well-known within Mesopotamian memory. Apparently it was an extremely severe but local flood. 'The earth' of Genesis 6–9 appears to be the Mesopotamian valley-territory in which the entire ecological system was destroyed.

This genealogy first shows the connection between Shem and Abraham; the promises of Genesis 9:26 and 27 are being kept. It shows too that the human race had plenty of time to save itself if it could. But it could not lift itself out of its wickedness and out of the dominion of death. God had to start doing something – and He started with Abraham.

Terah married at least two wives (Genesis 20:12). He must have been born about 135 years before Abraham was born. (The ages are difficult to understand. Either the family's years are 'carried forward' in some way so the ages accumulate from previous generations. Or we have miraculous extensions of people's ages. When these ages are better understood I suspect it will turn out that more than one factor will be involved in the explanation. For the moment we shall take the ages as they stand and not worry too much about their strangeness.)

Haran and Nahor were, it seems, Abraham's elder brothers. At some time before Abraham was 75 years old, Terah left Ur. The son Haran married in Ur and had two daughers, but then died at a time when the family were still living in Ur. Nahor married one of his nieces. Abraham married his half-sister, Sarai.

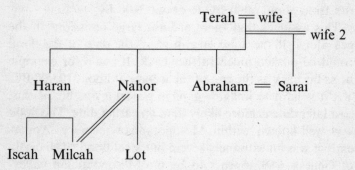

At some time before Abraham's seventy-fifth year the family moved to Haran (the two words 'Haran' are not the same; in Hebrew they are spelled differently). Then Terah died at 205 years. Abraham was about 75 years old (Genesis 12:4). Abraham had been called to leave Ur (see Acts 7:4; Genesis 15:6), but it was only after Terah's death that there was opportunity for him to follow God's summons.[1] Abraham was called to keep travelling. He took with him Sarai and Lot.

If Abraham was born at about 2000 BC, Terah's dates are 2135–1925 BC, and Abraham lived about 2000–1850 BC. It seems that their ages were miraculously extended.

But the signifiance of all of this is that we can see Abraham came from a pagan family. Ur and Haran were well-known as centres of moon-worship. Abraham's family and no doubt Abraham himself in his childhood *'worshipped other gods'* (Joshua 24:2).

Abraham is the most important figure in the Bible after Jesus. Christians are the *'children of Abraham'* (Galatians 3:29), and Abraham is the father of all believers, Jewish and Gentile.

Abraham is important because he is the model 'believer', the pattern of faith that God wants from us. Christians believe God in the same way that Abraham believed God.

Abraham is God's answer to sin. Humankind was excluded from paradise and had experienced the judgement of the flood. Neither would ever be repeated. But man is still rising up in rebellion against God. Does God have any other answer? Yes, He will send a Saviour, and the Saviour will be *'the seed of Abraham'*.

God's answer is Jesus! Jesus will be the answer to this rising rebellion. Jesus will be the answer to Nimrod, the answer to man's hatred of God. Jesus will be the one who unites, the answer to multinational apostasy. Jesus will bring forgiveness of sins, and will make possible a change in the hearts of men and women. It will be Jesus who brings men and women together. By His death and resurrection and heavenly throne He still is the answer.

The fall brought alienation from God, and hatred among men and women. Soon demonic strongholds were found in the human race. The flood wiped out a major civilisation and gave Noah's seed a second chance, but the godly examples of Enoch and Noah and the terrible deterrent of the flood brought no lasting change. So God sent Abraham, God's model-believer. He was used by God to demonstrate what it would mean to come to saving faith. He would persist in faith and so inherit God's promises to him. He would obey God without the Mosaic law or any other law, hearing God's voice directly. Eventually God would take an oath and say *'Now I know that you fear me; I will indeed bless you'*. And from that point on God would *'remember His holy covenant, the oath He swore to ... Abraham'*, until Abraham's seed should come, *'to rescue us from the hand of our enemies, and to enable us to serve Him without fear, in holiness and righteousness before Him all our days'* (see Luke 1:72–75).

## Footnote

[1] Acts 7:4 says that Abraham left after Terah's death. Genesis 11:26, 32; 12:4 contradicts this only if Abraham is reckoned as the eldest son, but Abraham is probably mentioned first because of importance not because of his being the oldest. In Acts 7 God appears first to Abraham in Ur (7:2); Genesis 12 does not say when the first call came. Modern people tend to read ancient books more in chronological order than they really were and so we tend to take Genesis 12 as meaning that the call came in Haran. But the text does not say that and it is a modern way of reading a text. Ancient readers (picking up a hint from Genesis 15:6!) placed the call in Ur, as does Stephen (in Acts 7:2–4), Philo (in *De Migratione Abrahami*, 176–177) and Josephus (in *Antiquities*, 1:154). Joshua 24:2–3 and Nehemiah 9:7 give a similar impression. Genesis 15:7 says *'I brought you ... out of Ur'*, not 'out of Haran'.

If you have enjoyed this book and would like to help us to send a copy of it and many other titles to needy pastors in the **Third World**, please write for further information or send your gift to:

**Sovereign World Trust**
**PO Box 777, Tonbridge**
**Kent TN11 0ZS**
**United Kingdom**

or to the **'Sovereign World'** distributor in your country.

| DATE | ISSUED TO |
| --- | --- |
|  |  |
|  |  |
|  |  |
|  |  |